WALKS IN OSCAR WILDE'S LONDON

WALKS IN OSCAR WILDE'S LONDON

Choral Pepper
Maps by Denis Thompson

PEREGRINE SMITH BOOKS

SALT LAKE CITY

For my mother, Lucille Iredale Carleson

This is a Peregrine Smith Book, published by Gibbs Smith, Publisher
P.O. Box 667
Layton, UT 84041

Cover production by Larry Clarkson
Interior production and maps by Roy Clark

Cover photos:
Oscar Wilde, 1882, by Napolean Sarony, courtesy of the National Portrait Gallery, London.
Hyde Park Corner and Rothschild Row, West Picadilly—both from turn-of-the-century picture postcards.

Manufactured in the United States of America

Library of Congress Cataloging-in-Publication Data

Pepper, Choral.
Walks in Oscar Wilde's London / Choral Pepper.
p.   cm.
Includes bibliographical references and index.
ISBN 0-87905-445-X (pbk.) : $12.95
1. Wilde, Oscar, 1854-1900—Homes and haunts—England—London.
2. London (England)—Social life and customs—19th century.
3. London (England)—Description—Tours. 4. Literary landmarks—England—London. 5. Walking—England—London.
I. Title.
PR5823.P47 1992
820.9'008—dc20   91-37926
CIP

Other titles in the Peregrine Traveler Series:

Walks in Gertrude Stein's Paris

Paris Portraits, Renoir to Chanel
Walks on the Right Bank

Walks in Picasso's Barcelona

HOW TO USE
THIS BOOK

Our focus in this book is to bring alive for the reader the London personalities, the culture, and the glitter of the ofttimes-wicked late-Victorian era that Oscar Wilde exemplified more profoundly than any other person. We would like to stress the importance of reading the book from beginning to end before starting on your walks. In recounting the adventures of our colorful nineteenth-century personalities, we followed their careers in sequence as they progressed, frequently moving from one neighborhood to another. By reading single chapters at random, you will miss the book's upwardly mobile trend and the amusing or scandalous incidents that motivated its characters' moves.

A second reason for reading the book through is that each of the eight districts covered has a distinct appeal. Should your time be too limited to enjoy all of the walks, an inclusive first reading will help you to determine which walks coincide best with your individual interests.

We had expected to include London's major museums in the walks, but our own experience proved that this was too much. Therefore we have mentioned in the narrative the museums in which items, works of art, or portraits of Victorian personalities may be seen on separate visits. There is no entrance charge to London's splendid museums. We particularly recommend the Victoria and Albert Museum, the Tate Gallery and the National Portrait Gallery, all of which include displays relating to our period. Visits to smaller, neighborhood museums like Leighton House and the Wallace Collection are included in the walks.

It was Dr. Samuel Johnson, famed for his dictionary, who wrote: "When a man is tired of London, he is tired of life; for there is in London all that life can afford." Oscar Wilde never tired of either. His spirit is an excellent guide.

Oscar Wilde in London, by Ming Lowe.

CONTENTS

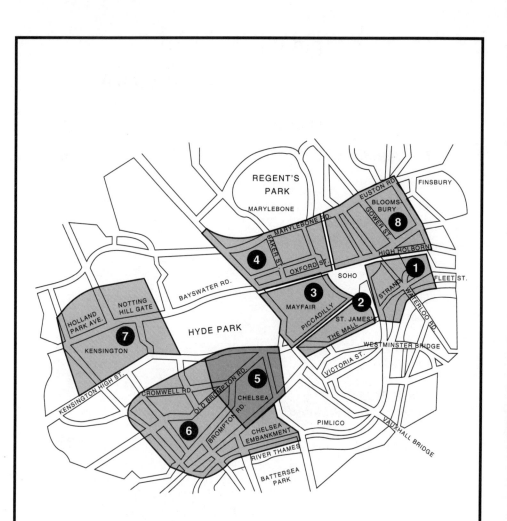

The general location of each of the eight walks in Oscar Wilde's London.

INTRODUCTION: WILDE AND HIS LONDON

It was a time when aristocrats switched beds as if they were playing musical chairs, when sartorial elegance had reached its peak, when scandal meant social alienation forever, and when all society adhered to a wicked writer's observation that "the best way to get the better of temptation is just to yield to it." (So long as one yielded discreetly.) It was the time of Oscar Wilde.

The reign of the abstinent Queen Victoria, who cloaked herself in mourning for forty years, was dominated by four highly romantic personalities: her bon vivant son, the Prince of Wales, who failed to emulate the somber perfection of his father; the beauteous Lillie Langtry, who was the prince's first officially recognized mistress; the enigmatic Oscar Wilde, who billed himself as an art critic and professor of aesthetics; and the eccentric, style-setting, expatriate American, James Abbott

Her Majesty, Queen Victoria.

McNeill Whistler, most famous for his portrait of his mother.

Until Albert Edward, Prince of Wales (subsequently to become King Edward VII) married his Danish princess, Alexandra, and gained a semblance of independence, the strata of society under Queen Victoria were stringently defined—the aristocracy and the masses. Lively Bertie, helped by the Industrial Revolution, changed all that.

Upon returning from a week-long honeymoon in the queen's gloomy Osborne House at Cowes, the young couple moved into London's Marlborough House, the great cut-stone and brick edifice on Pall Mall. Suddenly gaslight glared from every window. Music rippled through its halls. Ladies twirled to waltzes and flirted behind feathered fans. Scandalous rumors incited raised eyebrows among Victoria's grim guests up the Mall at Buckingham Palace—rumors such as one about Princess Alexandra proving on a dare that she could turn cartwheels so fast her ankles wouldn't show!

That was only the beginning. Soon the novelty of the Danish princess's gymnastic prowess and her adolescent apple-dunking games grew ho-hum. Bertie and his pals went in search of more sophisticated entertainment. Thus the illustrious "Marlborough Set" was born.

Princess Alexandra with her escort at the opening of a museum in 1884, as illustrated in the London News. *The Prince of Wales (in the beard) is behind her.*

Now all class lines crossed. Socializing with actresses like the visiting Sarah Bernhardt, artists like John Millais and Jimmy Whistler, poets like W.B. Yeats and Oscar Wilde, intellectuals, rich industrialists, American millionaires, and beautiful women like Lillie Langtry, no matter what their birthright, became de rigueur. Social acknowledgment by the Prince of Wales opened every door in London, except that of Buckingham Palace, where a scowling Victoria clung tenaciously to her morals and her manners.

After a few years the unfortunate Alexandra's defective hearing became a social obstacle. She chose to retire to the nursery with her children and resignedly closed her eyes to the romantic *affaires* of her princely husband. The beautiful Jersey Lily, although far from his first conquest, became the Royal's first officially recognized mistress. It was love at first sight for the prince and it lasted a good four years. Lillie, who had arrived in London from the British island of Jersey with her incompetent, alcoholic husband, also won the loyalty of another newcomer to London, Oscar Wilde.

Whether Lillie's celebrity as a reigning beauty launched Wilde's notoriety as a social wit, or whether Wilde's wit and laudatory writings about her established her legendary fame, is debatable. In truth their reputations fed upon each other. The finales of their careers carried them far apart, but in history Lillie's name is as irrevocably linked with Oscar Wilde's as it is with that of Edward Albert, Prince of Wales. Lillie was the catalyst who brought them all together.

During his lifetime of forty-six years, no one who spoke the English language was as consistently lighthearted and unmaliciously amusing as Oscar Wilde. He was the son of William Wilde, an established aural surgeon in Dublin who was knighted in 1863, and an Irishman who held a lifelong belief in the health-giving qualities of strong ale. His mother, a tall, stately socialist named Jane Francesca Elgee, wrote inflammatory articles under the pseudonym "Speranza." Oscar Wilde was born on October 16, 1854, and christened Oscar Fingal O'Flahertie Wills Wilde. Later he claimed that "a name which is destined to be in everybody's mouth must not be too long," so, like a balloonist shedding unnecessary ballast in order to rise, Oscar eventually settled on a single first name.

In 1864, as if portending the later fate of his son, Sir William Wilde's overactive libido led to the ruination of his reputation. The flagrant seduction of a willing patient named Mary Travers resulted in extortion, threats, scurrilous pamphlets, and finally a devastating lawsuit won by the plaintiff, whose counsel described her as a "bleeding, brokenhearted woman."

Dr. Wilde died in the spring of 1876, leaving Oscar a small property worth about four thousand pounds and his wife about seven thousand pounds, a relative pittance. Though the technical cause of his death is unknown, it is almost certain that he died because he no longer cared to live.

Oscar, meanwhile, graduated from Oxford, leaving in a blaze of glory when his poem "Ravenna" won the Newdigate Prize for that year. He came down from Oxford to London in the early months of 1879, having assured friends left behind that he had no ambition to become an Oxford don. "I'll be a poet, a writer, a dramatist," he vowed. "Somehow or other I'll be famous, and if not famous, I'll be notorious."

Although no one was prepared to hoist a welcoming flag, Lillie Langtry had already been apprised of his imminent arrival. While she was being introduced to London society at a "Sunday evening" held at the Belgravia home of Lady Sebright, a popular artist named Frank Miles had succumbed to temptation and sketched the new beauty on an envelope which was in his pocket.

"I'm no Millais nor Whistler," he explained as he worked, "just a popular artist who does pencil and pen-and-ink drawings for newspapers and magazines—always of beautiful women. That's why I *must* do you: to make London aware of the supreme beauty hiding in its midst."

"I haven't been hiding, Mr. Miles. I came here with my husband almost a year ago."

"Then where have you been? You must meet a friend of mine who is coming down from Oxford. His name is Oscar Wilde. He'll go mad over you. He writes poetry and he's extraordinary in every way. A genius." As he finished the sketch, he presented the envelope to Lillie with his address clearly marked. "I've never done this before," he assured her. "I never, never work out of my studio. You must come to me. But remember that name: Oscar Wilde."

Lillie remembered. She also remembered Frank Miles's address near the Strand. When Oscar Wilde arrived to share rooms with his friend at 13 Salisbury Street, Lillie's beauty had already been immortalized in several Frank Miles portraits, as well as by other artists.

It was the drama Oscar Wilde imparted to their relationship that set Lillie apart from the other great beauties of her day. He dedicated poems to her. He lavishly displayed symbolic lilies, even wearing one in his buttonhole. He camped on her doorstep on a cold night to prove his devotion to her (and draw attention to himself). While Oscar may have exploited his friendship with Lillie, his loyalty never wavered. When later events caused the social tide to turn temporarily against her, Oscar was there for support.

Meanwhile Lillie introduced him into the prestigious circles that provided an audience for his outrageous wit. Soon he was lionized, challenging American artist Jimmy Whistler's reputation for sly repartee. While Oscar plotted plays not yet produced, he edited a popular publication called *Woman's World* that helped to establish his name. He wrote reviews for the *Pall Mall Gazette*. His short stories appeared in the *Court and Society Review*. His epigrams were on every tongue. He may have played the fool, but nobody was fooled about his intellect. Scholars admired his grasp of Greek literature and art. Politicians and statesmen quoted his witty remarks. Probably no other man of his time was more widely acquainted in London.

With his intense appreciation for beauty, Oscar was a true Libra—and more, even balancing the scales sexually. Until after his marriage to Constance, it is doubtful that he understood his homosexual tendencies. Considering the moral laxity of the time, they might have been overlooked had he not broken the one cardinal rule—he was indiscreet. Scandal, the unforgivable Victorian sin!

However, as a guide to the glittering late-Victorian period in London, the spirit of Oscar Wilde opens more doors than can any other of his time. "I never travel without my diary," one of his dramatic characters once said. "One should always have something sensational to read in the train." Exploring Oscar Wilde's London is a bit like sneaking a peek at that diary.

WALK
THE STRAND
AND
COVENT GARDEN
ONE

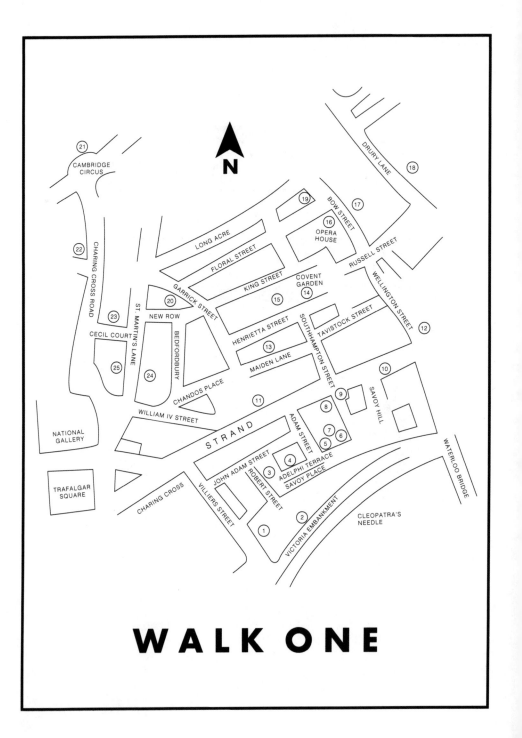

WALK ONE

When asked why he chose to live in London's West End, Oscar Wilde declared "a gentleman never goes east of Temple Bar." Consequently all of our walks take place in the West End of London.

Oscar Wilde came to live in London in 1879. Income from his inherited property in Ireland helped to support quarters off the Strand at 13 Salisbury Street, which he shared with the artist Frank Miles, whom he had known at Oxford. That house, "untidy and romantic" according to Lillie Langtry, was characterized by serpentine hallways, shadowy corners and awkwardly shaped rooms. Wilde aptly named it Thames House, since it provided a glimpse of the river. The house no longer stands, but it played an important role in Oscar Wilde's London debut, so it is worth a description.

The Strand, after Oscar Wilde's time. Salisbury Street, where Wilde lived with Frank Miles just off the Strand, is now gone.

There were three floors. Miles's studio occupied the top floor, Wilde had the floor below, and the ground floor was let to a student. Wilde's quarters consisted of a long, narrow, paneled sitting room painted entirely white. Blue china vases filled with fresh lilies graced every flat surface, and an easel holding Edward Poynter's portrait of Lillie Langtry dominated the room.

Tall, blond and handsome Frank Miles on the top floor restricted his work to drawing rather than painting, having once confessed to Lillie Langtry that he was color-blind. Possibly his affliction had sharpened his sense of contrast. Adept at rendering his subjects more handsome than they actually were, he was in great demand as a society artist and had been instrumental in initiating the mid-Victorian phenomena of P.B.s (Professional Beauties).

Never before nor since has there been a rage like the P.B.s, as they were called. No ordinary mortals posing for a fee, these ladies! No, these Professional Beauties were drawn from London's top social strata, the aristocracy. The modern context of the word "professional" is misleading. To have been paid would have been vulgar. Only the artists, like Miles, profited. Recognition for having been selected as a P.B. was reward in itself. Reproductions of the beauties appeared in every store window and hung in every middle-class dwelling. The originals graced the mansions of wealthy patrons of the arts. Queen Victoria's youngest son, Prince Leopold, became so enamored of a pen-and-ink sketch of Lillie Langtry he had seen while visiting Miles's studio that he acquired it to hang in his bedchamber—until his mother snatched it down.

The Wilde and Miles domicile on Salisbury Street soon provided a nucleus for a salon. Wilde's wit attracted intellectuals; Miles's talent attracted Professional Beauties. And where came the beauties, the Prince of Wales followed. Thames House habitués included artists like Jimmy Whistler and Edward Burne-Jones, royalty like Princess Louise and Prince Leopold, aristocracy like Lady Lonsdale, and visiting celebrities like Sarah Bernhardt, who autographed one of the white panels of Wilde's wall and in a playful mood made a mark to prove how high she could kick.

London's stage legends Dame Ellen Terry and her leading man, Sir Henry Irving, the first actor to be knighted, were frequent callers. After witnessing one of their performances at the Lyceum, Wilde dedicated a sonnet to Ellen, in part:

In the lone tent, waiting for victory,
She stands with eyes marred by the mists of pain,
Like some wan lily overdrenched with rain;

Ellen wrote later in her life: "The most remarkable men I have ever known were Whistler and Oscar Wilde. This does not imply that I like them better or admired them more than others, but there was something about both of them more instantaneously individual and audacious than it is possible to describe."

Other Wilde associates who gave this late-Victorian era so much flavor we shall meet later, as we explore Oscar Wilde's London. The most prized and frequent guest of Thames House, however, was Wilde's newly adopted idol, Lillie Langtry, in whose honor he initiated his illustrious lily trademark. (After he became famous, Wilde denied that he had actually made a practice of strolling along Piccadilly carrying a lily, but said that the fact people *believed* he had— and it was the kind of thing that he alone would have done— was a satisfying achievement because it had established a reputation based on fantasy.)

Charing Cross Station

On this walk we shall stroll through districts known as the Strand and Covent Garden, beginning at the ornate, monumental Charing Cross Station, opened in 1887. Here, amid a yeasty mixture of hotels and restaurants, lies the heart of London's performing-arts world, where Oscar Wilde, George Bernard Shaw, and Gilbert and Sullivan made their marks in the late 1800s. Great theatre has been a London tradition since Shakespeare, and for real quality, it is still unsurpassed, as are the design and magnificence of London's nineteenth-century theatres.

Extending from the east side of the station is Villiers Street, which leads to the Victoria Embankment and the district known as the Adelphi, which runs alongside the River Thames.

1. Residence of Rudyard Kipling
43 Villiers Street

Upon arriving in London from India in 1889 with fewer pounds in his pocket than he later cared to remember, Rudyard Kipling took three rooms on the second floor of this building. In his autobiography, *Something of Myself,* he called the street "primitive and passionate in its habits and population. My rooms were small, not over-clean or well-kept, but from my desk I could look out of my window through the fan-lights of Gatti's Music-Hall entrance, across the street, and almost onto its stage. The Charing Cross trains rumbled through my dreams on one side, the boom of the Strand on the other, while, before my windows, Father Thames under the Shot Tower walked up and down with his traffic."

Kipling wrote his *Barrack-Room Ballads and Other Verses,* and his novel *The Light That Failed* here. He found the English climate difficult after having lived in India and left in 1891 for warmer climes, returning to London in 1896 with an American wife.

Wilde's only recorded comment about Kipling was made in reference to his *Captains Courageous,* which relates a lad's adventures among the codfishermen off Newfoundland. "I really don't know why an author should write a book about cod-fishing . . . but perhaps," Wilde added ruminatively, "it is because I never eat cod." On another occasion he may have been referring to Kipling's writing style when he commented, "It is better to take pleasure in a rose than to put its root under a microscope."

Kipling's obituary when he died in 1936 read: "His coffin was borne by the Prime Minister, the Admiral of the Fleet, one field marshal, one classical scholar, the editor of the *Morning Post* and, of course, his agent, A.P. Watt, probably the saddest of them all."

2. The Victoria Embankment

As you wander around the corner from Kipling's address into the gardens of the Victoria Embankment, you will be treading a path walked by many great artists of the past. G.B. Shaw, James Barrie and John Galsworthy are among those who mused beside the reflection pond of the picturesque seventeenth-century York Water Gate, later incorporated into the Embankment gardens. This pride of the Victorians, completed in 1870, stands today as one of the most durable improvements ever made to London. The Embankment's bold engineering and ornate cast-iron street lamps were the talk of the day. The principal point of interest today is Cleopatra's Needle, a granite obelisk carved about 1450 B.C. in Egypt. It was presented to Britain in 1878 by Mohammed Ali, the viceroy of Egypt. Eager that their own civilization should prove as enduring, the Victorians buried a number of contemporary articles and mementos under the Needle before it was erected, among them a photograph of Oscar's dear friend, the celebrated beauty Lillie Langtry.

The Adelphi

Between the Strand and the river, just beyond Charing Cross Station, is an area called the Adelphi, built in the late eighteenth century by the Scottish "Brothers Adam," who created some of the finest architecture in London. This ambitious design involved streets, houses and terraces supported by an embankment of arches and subterranean vaults. Unfortunately the project resulted in the kind of financial fiasco suffered by some of our modern developments. A lottery was authorized by Parliament in 1773 to rescue the enterprise from disaster. Nevertheless the planned residential area attracted the elite of the day. Most of the elegant brick houses, embellished with exquisitely ornamented ceilings and matching patterned floors, and classical plaques, pilasters, arches and niches, have been demolished, but enough remain to give a taste of the time. A fine reconstruction of Brothers Adam architecture and décor from the Adelphi may be seen in the Victoria and Albert Museum.

3. Residence of Sir James Barrie and John Galsworthy
3 Robert Street

Following his divorce, Sir James Barrie moved from 100 Bayswater Road to a flat here on the third floor, with leaded casements looking south over the Embankment gardens. Barrie, who came to London from Scotland in 1885, made his name with *A Window in Thrums* and *The Little Minister*. He wrote two unsuccessful plays before he conquered the stage with *Quality Street*. Later, in 1904, his play *Peter Pan* was produced and has become a children's favorite to this day. His idea of fun was turning anything he saw or heard into an article worthy of publication. He claimed that he once paused by a bookstall and scanned a treatise on bridge building, then wrote "How I Built My Bridge over the Ganges" and got it published.

Of Barrie, Lady Nancy Astor once observed: "He got spoiled and lost all his homely Scottish ways after being taken up by the nobs. His cottage charm went and he became ridiculous." Other contemporaries said that he never recovered from the desolation caused by his wife leaving him for someone else.

Barrie's good friend, the novelist and playwright John Galsworthy, lived in the same building until he moved further out of London to Kensington. Galsworthy chiefly remembered his little Adelphi flat for its closeness to Barrie and their dinners at Romero's. Galsworthy established his reputation with *The Man of Property,* the first novel of his *The Forsyte Saga,* published in 1906. His portrait of late-Victorian and Edwardian upper-class commercial society has never been surpassed. According to a modern reviewer, "Galsworthy began as a critic of the upper-middle classes. He endures as their chronicler."

4. Residence of Richard D'Oyly Carte
4 Adelphi Terrace

At this address lived the great entrepreneur Richard D'Oyly Carte, the producer of Gilbert's and Sullivan's comic operas at the neighboring Savoy Theatre. Before moving in, he engaged Jimmy Whistler to oversee the interior design. In typical Whistler fashion the library walls were tinted primrose yellow to appear warm with sunshine even on London's foggy days, a scheme Wilde copied later when he moved into his own house in Chelsea.

Richard D'Oyly Carte, who promoted Gilbert and Sullivan in England and the U.S., (courtesy of the Savoy Hotel).

D'Oyly Carte began his career as a lecturer and theatrical agent. In 1875 he produced his first successful operetta, *Trial by Jury,* with lyrics by W.S. Gilbert and music by Sir Arthur Sullivan. This launched a partnership which prospered for some twenty years, even though Gilbert and Sullivan eventually only communicated with each other through their attorneys.

5. Residence of David Garrick
6 Adelphi Terrace

The great actor and theatre manager David Garrick, whose stage presence was still an influence a generation after his death, was among the earliest occupants of the Brothers Adam's Adelphi complex, living at this address on the Terrace.

6. Residence of Thomas Hardy
8 Adelphi Terrace

Thomas Hardy, poet and novelist, came to London in 1862 to study architecture. He both worked and lived in Sir Arthur Bloomfield's office at 8 Adelphi Terrace while learning the architect's vocabulary, which he used with great effect in *The Laodicean.* In thinking back about his Adelphi days, he said, "I sat there drawing inside the easternmost window of the front room on the first floor, occasionally varying the experience by idling on the balcony....the rooms contained fine Adam mantelpieces in white marble on which we used to sketch caricatures in pencil." After publishing *Under the Greenwood Tree,* he married and moved further out of the city. He was not comfortable in London, a city which he described as "a monster whose body had four million heads and eight million eyes." In 1881 he returned to his native Dorset, where he produced his masterpiece, *Tess of the D'Urbervilles.*

7. Residence of George Bernard Shaw
10 Adelphi Terrace

George Bernard Shaw moved to this fashionable address after marrying Charlotte Payne-Townshend, an heiress to whom the house was leased. Both over forty when wed, they settled down to a long, contented, businesslike, and unconsummated (according to Shaw) marriage in Charlotte's delightful rooms overlooking the river.

When Shaw became involved with the Fabian Society, a socialist organization, Charlotte helped the cause by sharing her house with the London School of Economics and Political Science, founded by Shaw's friends, the Webbs. The society's ideas on social engineering and political strategy eventually became the foundation of the British Labor party. Shaw's written propaganda greatly influenced the popularization of the socialist movement.

8. The Savoy Theatre
The Strand

(The Savoy Theatre was ravaged by fire in 1990, and is expected to reopen in 1992.)

This modish theatre on the Strand was built in 1881 by Richard D'Oyly Carte for the Gilbert and Sullivan operas. It was the first public building in London to be lighted by electricity. The opening production was *Patience*, the opera which satirized Oscar Wilde's dandyism with the familiar lines:

> *Though the philistines may jostle, you will rank as an apostle in the high aesthetic band,*
> *If you walk down Piccadilly with a poppy or a lily in your medieval hand.*

For his libretto for *Patience,* the opera that brought fame to the Gilbert and Sullivan collaboration, Gilbert found inspiration in the sequence of George Du Maurier caricatures of Wilde in *Punch.* Although other aesthetes—Whistler, Rossetti, Swinburne, and Ruskin—were equally involved in the movement, it was Wilde's exaggerations that prompted Gilbert to refer to him specifically in his parody. And, according to Max Beerbohm, it was that individualized portrait in *Patience* that prolonged the aesthetic movement and introduced it to America.

Gilbert astutely guessed that Wilde would appreciate the innocent fun of the parody and was rewarded with Wilde's hearty laughter. (The only thing worse in the world than being talked about, Wilde often claimed, was not being talked about.)

Among the good stories told about Gilbert is one that occurred during a rehearsal, when the brusque Gilbert, anxious to speak to a particular actress, asked a stagehand where she might be found.

"She's round behind," the stagehand replied.

"Yes, I know that," growled Gilbert, "but where is she?"

Sir Arthur Sullivan, the music maker of the team, had an ear so sensitive that it saved him one night when, returning to his home after a convivial party, he couldn't identify his own terrace house among the row of identical dwellings. He walked along the row kicking the metal shoe scrapers that stood beside the front doors. One rang a familiar note. Sullivan kicked it again. "That's it, E-flat," he muttered, and staggered confidently into his house.

9. The Savoy Hotel
The Strand

The Savoy, still an elegant and classy hotel, adjoins the theatre on the Strand. Built by D'Oyly Carte in 1889—the first London hotel to have numerous bathrooms, electric elevators and lights—it maintains a historic reputation for fine food. When it opened, D'Oyly Carte brought Ritz from Monte Carlo to take charge, and Ritz imported Escoffier to make history in the kitchen. Then followed as maître d' the celebrated Joseph, he of the luminous eyes, bushy brows, tiny mustache and long curly hair falling from a bald pate, whose recognition was almost as essential to one's social standing as that of the Prince of Wales.

One of the incidents contributing to the Oscar Wilde/Lord Alfred Douglas scandal that ruined Wilde's career occurred in the Savoy Hotel. While he had rooms there for

An advertisement depicting the Savoy Hotel in 1889, shortly before it opened, (courtesy of the Savoy Hotel).

convenience during rehearsals prior to the opening of one of his plays, his wife Constance arrived unexpectedly to bring mail and found him ensconced with his lover Douglas. When she besought Wilde to come home, he pretended he had been away so long he had forgotten the number of his house. Constance smiled through her tears.

10. Simpsons in the Strand
The Strand

Almost adjacent to the Savoy Hotel is Simpsons in the Strand, a London institution with the aura of a gentleman's club that opened in 1904. Reservations for dining may be made in the dignified entrance foyer graced with nineteenth-century portraits. In its various dining rooms, tables are covered with snowy white damask, and special waiters wheel silver-lidded carts to your table to serve joints of roast beef, Yorkshire pudding and strong horseradish sauce. Décor is quietly elegant eighteenth century, with paneled and painted woodwork in Wedgwood pinks and grays behind a row of paintings hung high under a plastered Adam ceiling. The fare is expensive.

11. The Adelphi Theatre
The Strand

Across the Strand from the Savoy is the old Adelphi Theatre, which Wilde booked in 1881 to produce his first play, *Vera*, in which the plot depended on Russian nihilism. He then proceeded to betray his apolitical innocence by carefully explaining, "Modern nihilistic Russia, with all the terror of its tyranny and the marvel of its martyrdoms, is merely the fiery and fervent background in front of which the persons of my dream live and love." With the play in rehearsal, the sister of the Prince of Wales's wife, who was married to Russian Tsar Alexander II, suddenly became a widow when the tsar was assassinated. Interest in nihilism soared. An opening date was set, but then something happened. The play never opened. A most likely explanation is that Wilde withdrew it in consideration for the feelings of the Prince and Princess of Wales, as Wilde was far too canny at that stage of his career to risk distressing one so important to his social aspirations.

Continue east along the Strand to Wellington Street and turn left.

The Adelphi Theatre, where Wilde's first play closed before it opened.

12. The Lyceum Theatre
Wellington Street

Closed now, with inane graffiti scribbled over its stately pillars, the once-fashionable Lyceum Theatre in Wellington Street was synonymous with the brilliant actors Sir Henry Irving and Dame Ellen Terry from 1874 to 1901. Ellen Terry, Irving's leading lady both on stage and privately, was often praised by Wilde, but it was G.B. Shaw who fell in love with her. "Ellen Terry is the most beautiful name in the world; it rings like a chime through the last quarter of the nineteenth century," Shaw wrote.

Although he attended her performances and they carried on a passionate correspondence, in typical Shavian style they never physically consummated their relationship. The "literate" romance went on for years before Shaw would even allow a meeting. In a letter to her, he explained his behavior thus: "Oscar Wilde said of me, 'An excellent man; he has no enemies; and none of his friends like him.'" He apparently felt more secure from a distance, although later he may have regretted this decision. In 1900 he wrote, "Still I have to dream of my Ellen and never touch her." They did finally meet when she performed in one of his plays. By then he was safely married.

Turn left off Wellington at Tavistock Street and proceed west into Maiden Lane.

13. Rules
35 Maiden Lane

Halfway up Maiden Lane on the north side stands a creamy yellow building with a red awning and a large brass shield on a column by the double front door. This is Rules, the famed theatrical restaurant. Its polished brass plate still proclaims that it serves luncheons, dinners and late suppers, and that it features the choicest vintage wines, liquors, spirits and cigars of the finest quality. With its comfortable Victorian furnishings and excellent English food, it was a favorite eating spot of the Prince of Wales, who had a private alcove in which to dine. Through the years, after Lillie Langtry had achieved fame as an actress, she frequently dined here with the prince when she returned from her American tours. By then they had become friends rather than lovers. Their signed portraits hang here yet.

Rules is still popular with royalty and VIPs, mostly English, who act as if it is their private club. It is doubtful that house specialties have changed since Dickens used to dine here in the 1860s, but the venison, oysters, game birds and fish from the cold North Sea are far more pricey today. Rules has a cover charge, does not accept credit cards and is closed in August.

Retrace your steps as far as Southampton Street and turn left.

14. Covent Garden

Covent Garden was the first planned urban development in London. It was here, in its former flower market, that Wilde shopped daily for the flashy lapel flowers that became his trademark. Here, also, the artist John Millais sent a servant to buy a Jersey lily for Lillie Langtry to hold while he painted her famous portrait named *The Jersey Lily,* which was exhibited in the Royal Academy show of 1878.

Until traffic congestion prompted its move to another location in 1974, the old central produce market was excitingly alive in the wee hours when everyone else was asleep. Today, under a glass roof that resembles a gigantic quonset hut, specialty food and craft stalls, trendy shops, and street entertainers have replaced lorries laden with fruit and flowers, and porters noisily unloading stout sacks, crates and barrels filled with the colors and scents of the old marketplace. Still Covent Garden is lively and fun, and a glimpse of the past may be experienced at the London Transport Museum on the southeastern corner of the square, with its extensive collection of carriages, real stagecoaches, buses and trains, or in the Theatre Museum next door, with its memorabilia from stars and playwrights from the gaslit past.

The charming maze of streets and tiny half streets surrounding Covent Garden comes as a delight to those seeking photogenic atmosphere. It is quite impossible to chart a turn-left, turn-right course among them. The district is relatively small, so the best way to enjoy it is simply to weave back and forth in the general area designated on your map. You are bound to hit the most significant landmarks. Among them are:

15. St. Paul's Church
Covent Garden

Behind Covent Garden's old market building stands St. Paul's Church (not to be confused with St. Paul's Cathedral), called the "actor's church" because so many famous stage celebrities have been put to rest here. When the Duke of Bedford, heir to the land, commissioned architect Inigo Jones in 1630 to lay out a square with a church at one end, he asked for an inexpensive building. Inigo Jones complied by designing what he called the "handsomest barn in Europe." St. Paul's still has its original eastern portico with the Tuscan arches. The church entrance is on the far side, at Inigo Place, which runs into Bedford Street. The churchyard between King Street and Henrietta Street is still lit by gaslights decorated with a ducal coronet in honor of the dukes of Bedford. Inside the church (closed on Sundays) are many memorials to actors, among which are the ashes of Oscar Wilde's loyal friend Ellen Terry, who died in 1928. During his trial and period of disgrace, she was one of the few who stood by him and aided him financially.

An amusing incident occurred during Ellen Terry's funeral. Leading the long parade of mourners in the procession to the church were Ellen's son Teddy and her daughter Ely, who had been bitterly estranged for years, not only from each other but from other relatives as well. Now, however, as all the enemies walked together arm in arm, Teddy excitedly erupted in a voice heard by all, "We must have *more* occasions like this!" Hilda Barnes, the devoted nurse who had cared for Ellen in her last years, restrained chuckles all through the funeral ceremony, thinking how Ellen Terry would have laughed at that line.

6. The Royal Opera House
Bow Street

On the northeast corner of Covent Garden stands the Royal Opera House with its gigantic columns and classical pediments. Inside, gilded tier upon tier of rococo boxes and galleries radiate from either side of the royal box, towering into an upper darkness. At the turn of the century, gala nights at the opera were organized by Lady de Grey. Men wore uniforms or court dress adorned with ribbons and medals, while the women preened in jewel-studded tiaras. Lady Londonderry, scanning the auditorium through lorgnettes, received her friends in one box. Lady Charles Beresford, whom they called the "Painted Lady" because of the array of colored chiffon scarves and beads draped around her neck, received in another.

After the opera, guests as well as performers might proceed to Lady de Grey's mansion, Combe Court, where Caruso would sing until dawn. Wilde greeted a new arrival at one of Lady de Grey's receptions with the exclamation, "Oh, I'm so glad you've come. There are a hundred things I want not to say to you!"

17. Bow Street Police Court
Bow Street

Across the street from the Opera House is the famed Bow Street Police Court, with its iron railing along the sidewalk. The first court opened here in 1740. In 1748 the famous playwright and novelist Henry Fielding and his half-blind brother Sir John became the presiding magistrates. It was a later playwright, Oscar Wilde, however, whose incarceration here without bail, following his arrest in Belgravia in 1893, marked the end for England's most illustrious nineteenth-century creative genius.

"With what a crash this fell!" Wilde wrote from his cell to friends Ada Levenson and Robert Sherard, comparing his plight to the situation in the Greek tragedy *Agamemnon.* Immediately following his arrest, Wilde's name was removed from the billboards at the two theatres where *An Ideal Husband* and *The Importance of Being Earnest* were playing. In America actress Rose Coghlan, who was about to take Wilde's play *A Woman of No Importance* on the road, canceled it. Few friends stood by, even in France where licentiousness was less severely condemned.

There, Colette's husband, the columnist "Willy," was highly amused by England's embarrassment. He registered his disapproval in *L'Echo de Paris,* pretending that homosexuality was only an English vice. At the same time, however, French journalist Henry Bauer defended Wilde, claiming that Wilde's heteroclite tastes were no one's affair. "Wilde has done no harm," he wrote. "Young Douglas was old enough to go out without his governess, and without his father's permission."

And indeed he was. Wilde had been introduced to the startlingly beautiful, twenty-one-year-old Lord Alfred Douglas, a recent dropout from his third year at Wilde's own alma mater, Magdalen College, when the aspiring young poet had come to London. His was an era of youth revolting against the trivial morality of the dying nineteenth century. Wilde, who as a student had vowed himself "to eat the fruit of all the trees in the garden of the world," was being rediscovered at Oxford. Thus it was no wonder Douglas found the more mature Wilde as fascinating as Dorian had found Lord Henry Wotton in Wilde's novel, *The Picture of Dorian Gray.* And Wilde, equally attracted by titles and beauty, found his cup running over as the incandescent Lord Douglas followed their introduction with a flood of letters and poems. The tumultuous passion that possessed them is inexplicable to heterosexuals, but through all the furies of anger, deceit and separation, it never seemed to leave them free.

Walk south on Bow Street and turn left on Russell. Continue down Russell Street into Drury Lane.

18. The Theatre Royal
Drury Lane

The handsome theatre you see today opened in 1812 and, although the fourth one to be built on this site, it is still the oldest playhouse in London. When the previous theatre was demolished by fire in 1809, its owner, the playwright Richard Sheridan (best known for his classic comedy, *The School for Scandal*) remarked while watching from a nearby tavern, "Leave me, leave me; 'tis a great pity if a man cannot take a glass of wine by his own fireside."

It is not surprising that Drury Lane's oversized stage has been the choice for the great modern musicals like *My Fair Lady* and *Miss Saigon,* considering that in the 1880s *Carmen* was produced on it with real bulls, and even earlier the stage was filled with live horses for a scene in *Henry V*. It is an elegant theatre in the best London tradition. If you attend a play, go early to admire the royal boxes before the lights dim.

Return to Bow Street. Turn left onto Floral Street, which runs alongside the stage door of the Opera House.

19. The Nags Head
Floral Street

If you are ready for a pub lunch, the Nags Head is conveniently located in the middle of Covent Garden. Its sign, featuring the head of a circus horse, has been hanging here since 1827. The décor is Victorian, with the old bar, Lincrusta ceiling and heavy moldings still intact. Usually the public room is crowded, but lunch is served upstairs, as is an early dinner for theatregoers.

Continue down Floral Street to Garrick Street.

20. The Garrick Club
15 Garrick Street

Where Floral dead-ends at Garrick Street, named for the eighteenth-century actor David Garrick who died in 1779, you will see an impressive, but unmarked, old gray stone building with ironwork trim on the south side of the street. This is the Garrick Club, as exclusive and popular with today's celebrities as it was in the 1800s, when it was organized for members involved in the theatre. Inside are a notable collection of theatrical paintings and a long table at which diners sit informally.

The Garrick Club was especially favored by Sir William Gilbert of Gilbert and Sullivan fame. Soon after the death of Sullivan, Gilbert chanced upon a woman attending a club function who obviously had not kept abreast of the news. Seeking a gambit to open a conversation with the famed lyricist, she asked him what his collaborator, the maestro, was doing.

"He's doing nothing," was Gilbert's answer.

"But surely he is composing?" persisted the questioner.

"On the contrary, madam," Gilbert snapped. "He is decomposing."

Another prominent member was William Makepeace Thackeray, the novelist best known for *Vanity Fair*. This gentleman once blackballed for membership someone named Hill, a self-made man with a strong cockney accent. "I blackballed him because he is a liar," Thackeray explained. "He calls himself 'ill' when he isn't."

Where Garrick Street runs into St. Martin's Lane, turn right and follow St. Martin's Lane north to West Street, which leads into Cambridge Circus.

21. The Palace Theatre
Cambridge Circus

The baroque terra-cotta façade and gilt-and-marble interior of the Palace Theatre, built in 1888, has been restored to its former grandeur by its new owner, composer Andrew Lloyd Webber of modern musical (*The Phantom of the Opera*) fame. Webber intends to turn the theatre into a "palace of music" with lunchtime performances.

In an earlier day Sarah Bernhardt, after reading Wilde's *Salomé,* determined to open the play in London, so she booked the Palace Theatre. After seeing her onstage for the first time, Wilde had rewritten the play in French as a vehicle for her. He was full of ideas. "I should like everyone on the stage to be in yellow," he said. Someone mentioned a violet sky. "A violet sky...yes...certainly a violet sky...and then in place of an orchestra, braziers of perfume. Think!" he dreamed aloud, "the scented clouds rising and partly veiling the stage from time to time...a new perfume for each emotion."

Sarah, meanwhile, had her own ideas. The play had been in rehearsal for three weeks when, in June 1892, the Lord Chamberlain refused a license on the ground that the play introduced biblical characters in violation of some ancient law. Highly indignant with the censor and furious with Wilde for not having applied for the license earlier, Bernhardt was fuming in her dressing room. "Do you mind if

Sarah Bernhardt, the famous French actress, who never played Salomé in London.

I smoke, madam?" asked the repentant Wilde. "I don't care if you burn," snapped Sarah.

Sarah never played *Salomé* in London.

22. The London Hippodrome
Charing Cross Road

Now turn back from Cambridge Circus onto Charing Cross Road and follow it south to my favorite London passageway, Cecil Court. En route you will pass the old London Hippodrome, an incredible Victorian gingerbread affair crowned with a knight mounted on a horse. It opened in 1900 with an aquatic show fed by a stream that ran under the theatre. Cast in this first production, *Giddy Ostend,* was an unknown comedian with a tiny part. His name was Charles Chaplin.

The stream was still lending glamor to dramatic stage sets as late as 1926, when vaudeville was popular. Apparently the stream eventually dried up, since today the building houses a disco and an underground station.

23. Cecil Court

Continue along Charing Cross Road to Cecil Court, a tiny, crowded "walk street" which runs from the east side of Charing Cross Road through to St. Martin's Lane. If printed memorabilia of the past holds any fascination for you, the tiny shops, featuring old books, prints, maps and documents, crowded along both sides of this passageway, represent a treasure trove. After musing through Cecil Court, exit onto St. Martin's Lane and turn right.

24. The Coliseum Theatre
St. Martin's Lane

The theatre lies on the east side of the street among a number of eighteenth- and nineteenth-century buildings which are still intact. Built in 1902 to rival the Drury Lane, its early playbills featured Ellen Terry, Lillie Langtry and Sarah Bernhardt at various times. Sarah Bernhardt particularly made a lasting impression when a friend, watching her do makeup for Cleopatra, was intrigued to see her painting the palms of her hands a terra-cotta red. "No one in the audience will possibly see that," commented Bernhardt's friend. "Maybe not," replied the actress, "but if I catch sight of my hands, then they will be the hands of Cleopatra."

25. The Salisbury
90 St. Martin's Lane

On the west side of St. Martin's Lane is another of our favorite pubs, The Salisbury, popular with actors performing in nearby theatres. Established in 1892, it was built on the site of Lord Salisbury's land and first was called Salisbury Stores. Its hand-carved mahogany, Lincrusta ceiling and old lamps were restored in 1962. Gold velvet settees fit cozily into alcoves, and it is a pleasant place to relax with a drink after perusing Cecil Court around the corner.

The Strand-Covent Garden walk ends where St. Martin's Lane exits into Trafalgar Square, a spot dominated by the National Portrait Gallery and National Gallery, which overlook the dramatic fountains and Landseer lions surrounding the column that supports the heroic Admiral Nelson.

Transportation by bus from here is convenient to most parts of inner London.

WALK

ST. JAMES'S

TWO

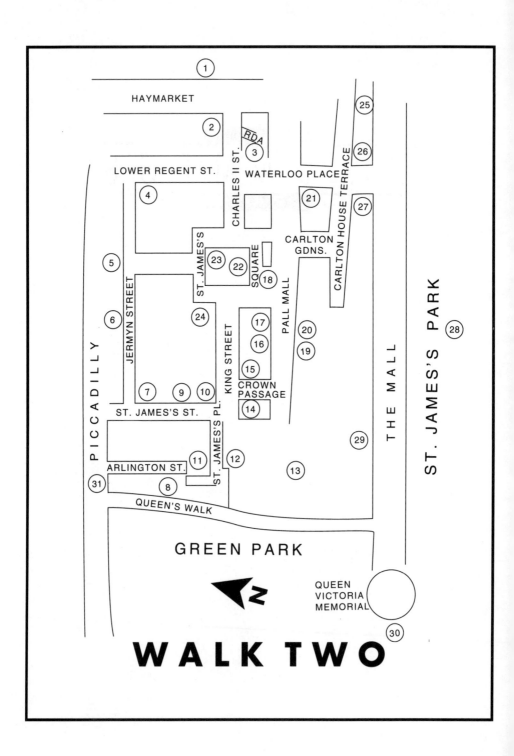

HAYMARKET

LOWER REGENT ST.

WATERLOO PLACE

CHARLES II ST.

RDA

CARLTON HOUSE TERRACE

ST. JAMES'S SQUARE

CARLTON GDNS.

PALL MALL

JERMYN STREET

KING STREET

ST. JAMES'S ST.

ST. JAMES'S PL.

ARLINGTON ST.

QUEEN'S WALK

CROWN PASSAGE

PICCADILLY

ST. JAMES'S PARK

THE MALL

GREEN PARK

N

QUEEN VICTORIA MEMORIAL

WALK TWO

The St. James's walk wends among a cluster of squares, lanes, narrow streets and cul-de-sacs lying south of Piccadilly and bordered by the Haymarket to the east, the Mall to the south, and Green Park to the west. It is an area long associated with royalty and especially noted for a plethora of gentlemen's clubs and bachelor apartments. (Beau Brummel, a St. James's dandy, took men out of knee breeches and put them into pants here at the turn of the seventeenth century.) In the nineteenth century a respectable lady wouldn't dare walk along its streets alone for fear any man she met might get the idea that she was trying to meet him.

Today St. James's remains a masculine stronghold, with shops representing the most elite of shirtmakers, hatters, boot makers, antique art dealers, wine merchants and investment companies.

Piccadilly Circus

Our walk begins on the south side of busy Piccadilly Circus. When you are pushing through the throngs that crowd Piccadilly at any hour, it takes some imagination to mentally transform the traffic noise of today's motor vehicles into the nineteenth-century clatter of wooden carriage wheels. It takes less, however, to mentally associate today's spiky-haired,

Picadilly Circus, near the turn of the century.

outrageously garbed rock stars with the flamboyant attire of an Oscar Wilde, strutting along Piccadilly carrying lavender gloves in one hand and a lily in the other. Sounds may have changed, but the throngs were ever so.

Speaking at the Travellers Club in Oscar Wilde's time, the celebrated explorer Joseph Thompson was relating his 1878 adventure in Africa when the expedition leader died, leaving the twenty-one-year-old Thompson to take over.

"Of all your adventures," asked J.M. Barrie, author of *Peter Pan,* "what was the most dangerous part?"

"Crossing Piccadilly Circus when I returned," vowed Thompson.

The name Piccadilly came into use during the time of Charles II, when only a few houses clung to this crossroad with the Haymarket. The most important was a small domain known as Piccadilly Hall and owned by one Robert Baker, who had become rich selling the stiff lace collars called pickadills you see worn in Queen Elizabeth I portraits.

Fourteen years after Wilde made his debut in London in 1879, the bronze Eros, god of love, was mounted on its pedestal on the Regent Street side of Piccadilly Circus. The bow and arrow of the statue, commemorating the Victorian philanthropist Lord Shaftesbury, were designed as a play on the Shaftesbury name. Society of the time was no less amused at the choice of the god of love as a tribute to a man considered so tiresome that it hardly shocked even prudish Victorians when his widow fell into the arms of an Italian envoy almost before the strains of the funeral dirge had faded away.

Leading from Piccadilly at an oblique angle to the southeast is the Haymarket, a street which attracts tasteful shoppers for rainwear to London's famous Burberrys and theatregoers to its two historic theatres.

1. The Haymarket Theatre
The Haymarket

This theatre played an important role in the progress of two colorful lives of the 1890s. It was here that Oscar Wilde's *An Ideal Husband* opened to rousing applause from the Prince of Wales in the royal box. George Bernard Shaw, who had just become drama critic for Frank Harris's *Saturday Review,* wrote with equal enthusiasm: "In a certain sense, Mr.

Wilde is to me our only thorough playwright. He plays with everything; with wit and philosophy, with drama, with actors and audience, with the whole theatre. Such a feat scandalizes the Englishman, who cannot anymore play with wit and philosophy than he can with a football or cricket bat."

The stage of the Haymarket Theatre was also the scene of Lillie Langtry's debut as a professional actress, following the traumatic turn her life had taken with the secret birth of her daughter, the end of her romance with the Prince of Wales, and the financial disaster experienced by her drunken husband. (More about this on the Mayfair walk.) Before disappearing from London society during her pregnancy, she had accepted a simple acting role to aid a charity fund-raising event sponsored by Henrietta Labouchere, a former actress married to a prominent member of Parliament.

When the energetic, stagestruck Mrs. Labouchere learned from Oscar Wilde of Lillie's return to London and her need to support herself, she, like Wilde, was so convinced of Lillie's potential as an actress that she volunteered to tutor the reluctant beauty for an amateur role at the matinee of another fund-raising production, this time performed by professionals. The play was *She Stoops to Conquer,* with Lillie in the role of Kate Hardcastle.

"After the matinee you'll qualify as a professional," Henrietta promised, "and the managers will pay you eighty pounds a week."

Considering Langtry's former social prestige and established fame as a beauty, Henrietta had no problem in selling the theatre management on hiring her for the entire run of the play. The Prince of Wales sent flowers and attended her first performance, as did a proud Wilde, who promised to write a play especially for her. Lillie Langtry was an unqualified success.

2. Her Majesty's Theatre
The Haymarket

On the west side of the Haymarket stands what many producers consider London's most remarkable theatre. In order to accommodate productions featuring both the devil in hell and angels in heaven, Herbert Beerbohm Tree designed the theatre in 1895 with understage mechanisms, in addition to the usual wings and overhead rigging which permitted characters like Peter Pan to fly through the air. It is this understage apparatus that contributed so grandly to the staging of the modern Webber musical, *The Phantom of the Opera*.

Actor and manager Sir Beerbohm Tree made a number of lasting contributions to the theatre. It was he who founded the great Royal Academy of Dramatic Art, which was begun in his theatre. He taught that "illusion is the first and last word of the stage. All that aids illusion is good, all that destroys illusion is bad," and warned that "scenes are embellishments which should not overwhelm the dramatic interest. If the balance is upset, illusion is gone. Good theatre," he observed, "achieves a balance between idealism and illusion." Tree would have been proud of Webber's *Phantom*.

Like Henry Irving with his Lyceum, Tree's theatre was his "home." The corroded copper dome that crowns its roof enclosed a wonderful replica of an ancient baronial banquet hall with great iron-clamped doors and paneled walls, in which he received guests for late suppers.

On Tree's acting ability, his good friend Wilde commented, "He doesn't act on the stage; he behaves," and found him more suited to character parts than to straight roles, but as a producer and director, Tree excelled. It was he who, during a rehearsal, decided that his actresses were projecting too worldly an attitude for their roles. "Now, ladies," he called up to the stage, "a little more virginity, if you please."

3. Royal Opera Arcade
The Haymarket

Across Charles II Street, around the corner from Her Majesty's Theatre, is New Zealand House, a modern high rise which incorporates the old Royal Opera Arcade on its ground floor, unchanged with its charming row of bow-fronted shops designed by Nash in 1817. Walk the short block west to Lower Regent Street, and then turn right to reach Jermyn Street.

4. Jermyn Street

This quietly charming thoroughfare is reminiscent of a more elegant era. Mixed in among Jermyn's fashionable shops to the west is Floris at number 89, a perfumer by appointment

to Her Majesty; Harvie and Hudson at number 97, renowned
shirtmakers with one of London's finest examples of a mid-
Victorian shopfront; and Paxton and Whitfield at number 93,
where countless varieties of cheese are sold over a wooden
counter. It was at a nearby florist's that Wilde pulled one of
his "absurdities" by asking the attendant to remove several
bunches of primroses from the window.

"With pleasure, sir. How many would you like to have?"

"Oh, I don't want any," Wilde replied. "I only asked to
have them removed from the window because I thought that
they looked tired." Determined to be talked about, Wilde
knew full well how such nonsense would make people
chatter. He soon got his reward. George Du Maurier began to
caricature him in *Punch*.

5. St. James's Church
Jermyn Street

Still favored for society weddings, the church was
bombed badly during World War II and only retains portions
of its earlier grandeur, namely the organ case, the altarpiece
of gilded wood with garlands of flowers, and the marble font
in the form of the tree of life, all carved by Grinling Gibbons
in the seventeenth century.

6. Site of Prince's Hall
Prince's Arcade

Adjacent to the churchyard is Prince's Arcade, extending
between Jermyn Street and Piccadilly. In the nineteenth
century a building on the Piccadilly end of the arcade housed
a lecture hall where the American Bret Harte always attracted
an enthusiastic audience. He had come to London in 1885 to
replenish his dwindling funds by selling revamped stories of
the American West to British magazines. A great favorite with
the English was "Plain Language from Truthful James," his tale
in verse about a plan to cheat the Chinese Ah Sin in a card
game, but by "ways that are dark," Truthful James is always
outwitted by the "heathen Chinee." Whistler, whose favorite
Harte story was "The Luck of Roaring Camp," entertained him
frequently, read some of Harte's stories at his famous
"breakfasts," and did much to promote his countryman.

Another popular lecturer in Prince's Hall was Oscar Wilde, following his return to London from his American tour. He titled his lecture "My Personal Impressions of America." Dressed in a Balzacian costume with tight pantaloons, a huge stock and his hair curled in a Neronian coiffeur, he startled his audiences at first sight, but his melodious voice and droll humor soon had them captivated. Among his impressions of America, he cited Salt Lake City in Utah as the highlight of his tour, saying that he had spoken in the opera house, which he described as a huge building about the size of Covent Garden which "holds with ease fourteen families." He thought polygamy prosaic: "How much more poetic it is to marry one and love many!"

In New Orleans he found the Blacks picturesque and was surprised that painters had paid so little attention to them as a subject for art. He also delighted in telling about going down into a mine in Leadville, Colorado, where he had imbibed whisky with the miners and opened a new vein with a silver drill, naming the lode "The Oscar."

His lecture was so successful that he took it on tour throughout the British Isles.

7. The Cavendish Hotel
Duke Street

Continue along Jermyn to Duke Street, another elegant reminder of earlier times. Here, on the corner of Jermyn and Duke Street, once stood the Cavendish Hotel, run by the "Duchess of Duke Street"—a title not due to birthright, but because the eccentric Rosa Lewis *earned* her reputation as an extraordinary Edwardian lady. A modern hotel of the same name lies further along on Jermyn Street.

Rosa didn't clear enough profit to open her own distinguished premise until 1900, about the same time as Wilde's tragic end in Paris, but she achieved her reputation and the means to acquire her hotel by catering to many of the aristocrats who had played host to Wilde. Her Cavendish Hotel was like no other. Closed to the public, it admitted only gentlemen personally acceptable to Rosa, and Rosa had discriminating taste. She hankered after titles.

The hotel was divided into suites, each with its own mahogany-encased bathtub and private dining room. The Prince of Wales kept a permanent suite, in which he could dine privately with whomever he wished. Moreover it opened onto a private courtyard through four doors by which hasty exits could be made in an emergency. When he entertained Lillie Langtry there in the 1900s, he had ascended to the throne and she had become an internationally recognized actress. Their desire for privacy at that stage in their relationship was oriented more toward reminiscing than pillow talk.

Rosa's expert cooking and caustic cockney wit kept the place humming for forty years. With her innate aversion to scandal, she never failed to advise her confidantes, of whom she had many, to burn all love letters. "No letters, no lawyers" was her sage advice.

Two gentlemen who maintained permanent suites were Sir William Eden, father of Anthony Eden, and Lord Ribbesdale, lord-in-waiting to Queen Victoria in 1880. Once when Lord Ribbesdale brought Rosa home from the theatre, friends called out to ask what the play had been like. "T'was the sort of play you'd take your cook to," she cracked back. Both permanent residents caused much comment and often appeared in public with the richly cloaked Rosa, but there is no concrete evidence that either of them was her lover. True to form, Rosa burned her own letters.

Continue west along Jermyn Street, crossing St. James's Street, to where it dead-ends at Arlington Street.

8. Residence of Lord Houghton
21 Arlington Street

It was at the Arlington home of Lord Houghton, an elderly widower and charming host, that Lillie Langtry inspired the oddest tribute of her career from the American poet Joaquin Miller, a man as purposefully unique and implausible as Oscar Wilde. Known as the "Byron of Oregon," the great interpreter of America burst upon London society dressed in fringed buckskin shirt and trousers like a road-company Buffalo Bill. He was a sensation.

"*You* are poetry!" he exclaimed upon meeting Lillie, awed at her startling beauty.

"Then write me a poem," she challenged jokingly, and moved along the reception line. Later she looked for him, but he seemed to have disappeared.

Then suddenly, toward the end of the evening, he

reappeared as dramatically as an explosion. "I've done it!" he announced, holding up a torn envelope. Then he cleared his throat and tugged at his beard in the expectant hush.

"To the Jersey Lily," he read, bowing to her.

If all God's world a garden were,
And women were but flowers,
If men were bees that busied there
Through endless summer hours,
O! I would hum God's garden through
For honey till I came to you.

He then presented her with the torn envelope, the only poem he ever wrote to a living woman.

Another American was present at that same party—the guest of honor, General Ulysses Grant. Lord Houghton introduced him as "the victorious leader of the Northern armies in the war against the Southern rebels some years ago," adding as he brought him to Lillie that the two of them fittingly represented Venus and Mars.

General Grant had been chosen by the host to escort Lillie to dinner. She exhausted herself trying to engage him in conversation, but he was curt and ill at ease. Finally in desperation she asked, "And what did you do after the war, General?"

"Served two terms as president of the United States, madam."

9. St. James's Street

Return to St. James's Street and turn right. At number 37, the elegant railings and entrance lamps mark White's, a private club founded in 1693 as a chocolate house. The bow window was added in 1811. White's is London's oldest club and its most famous, having provided a model for every other gentlemen's club in the city. No longer a rendezvous for chocolate drinkers who gamble, its clientele today leans toward hard-drinking Conservatives, in spite of the fact that the Prince of Wales once abandoned it for being "too stuffy" and started his own Marlborough Club.

Just down the street is Boodles at number 28. It was founded as a coffeehouse in 1762 and acquired its bay window in 1824. It was here that the gambling addiction of

Regency style setter Beau Brummel drove him into debt and forced him to flee to Paris to escape his creditors.

Number 69 on the west side of the street, now empty, was once the conservative Carlton Club, originally known as Arthur's. It was founded in 1832 by Arthur Wellesley, the Duke of Wellington, who once professed that railways were a dangerous evil because "they encouraged the working classes to move about." Lord Randolph Churchill often lunched here with his Tory friends while his American wife Jennie lunched at home with the Prince of Wales, which gave birth to rumors of an affair. Since they were both discreet, no writings ever turned up to prove the point, but they remained close lifelong friends.

The club was damaged during World War II and again in 1990, when it survived a terrorist bombing by the Irish Republican Army, in which injuries were suffered by several members. It has now been incorporated into rooms once part of White's Chocolate and Gaming House.

10. Pied-à-terre of Ian Malcolm
3 Pickering Place

On the left, through a paneled archway to the north of Berry Brothers and Rude Wine Merchants, is Pickering Place, built in 1731. To get a closer look, wait until you reach the bottom of St. James's Street, cross, and then walk back through the archway into the court. If the gate is closed, you will only know you are at Pickering Place by the number three. The quaint little dark-brick house standing behind a stone sculpture of Wellington in the court was presented by the Iron Duke (Wellington) to an ancestral Malcolm. In the mid-1900s it was inherited by Ian Malcolm, the unacknowledged son-in-law of Lillie Langtry—unacknowledged because when he married Lillie's daughter, Jeanne Marie, neither he, his noble family, nor her daughter would have anything more to do with Lillie, who had kept the true identity of Jeanne Marie's father secret until her wedding day. (More about this on the Mayfair walk.)

11. Residence of Oscar Wilde
10 St. James's Place

Pass Blue Ball Yard, then turn right onto St. James's Place. At the height of Wilde's success, he took a flat on this tiny street at number 10, opposite the charming Duke Hotel, in order to elude the curious eyes of his wife while he was engaged in his nefarious homosexual affairs. He did not elude the eyes of a curious porter, however, who took note of Wilde's visitors and later appeared as a witness against him at the infamous trial which sent Wilde to prison for two years.

12. Spencer House
St. James's Place

At the end of St. James's Place rises the Palladian grandeur of Spencer House, the London residence built by the Spencer ancestors of Lady Diana Spencer, who became the Princess of Wales in 1981.

13. St. James's Palace, Lancaster House and Clarence House
St. James's Street

At the end of St. James's Street, where it meets Pall Mall, lies the large compound enclosing St. James's Palace, Lancaster House and Clarence House. In spite of destruction and alterations, the palace still offers a fine example of brick Tudor architecture in its gatehouse and clock tower. Charles II, James II, Mary II, Anne and George IV were all born here.

After the old palace at Whitehall burned in 1699, St. James's Palace became the official residence of the monarch, until it gave place to Buckingham Palace. Foreign ambassadors are still posted to the "Court of St. James," however.

On January 22, 1901, eleven months before his sixtieth birthday, Albert Edward, Prince of Wales, finally became king. The traditional Accession Council was held at St. James's Palace, where the oath was administered by the Archbishop of Canterbury. In a spontaneous address the new king announced that he would drop his father's name—for there could only be one Albert—and be called Edward VII. Among intimates, of course, he was still known as Bertie.

The stucco-fronted mansion on the west side of the group of buildings was built by John Nash for the Duke of Clarence before he became King William IV. Then, before her accession, it was the London residence of Princess Elizabeth and the Duke of Edinburgh. Now it is the home of Queen Elizabeth, the Queen Mother.

Lancaster House, on the opposite side from Clarence

House, is now used for government receptions and conferences, but it was begun in 1825 for the Duke of York, who died before the house was completed, leaving enormous debts. In 1840 it was acquired by one of his creditors, the Marquess of Stafford (later Duke of Sutherland), who renamed it Stafford House. The magnificence of its state apartments led Queen Victoria to say to the Duchess of Sutherland, "I have come from my house to your palace!"

Millicent, the Duchess of Sutherland, was a half sister to Daisy Warwick, the Prince of Wales's officially recognized mistress who followed Lillie Langtry. Although Millie was not plagued with the untamable passions of her sister, she, too, knew romance. The man to whom she, shimmering in diamonds, discreetly offered her hand while greeting guests at the top of the staircase in Stafford House was handsome, secretive Lord Reginald Esher. This gentleman's genius lay in writing confidential memoranda for Queen Victoria, so he, like Millie, was a master of discretion. It is doubtful that his wife was aware of the throbbing of his heart as he exchanged a meaningful meet-me-in-the-garden look with the stunning lady in the tiara at the top of the stairs.

History only remembers Lady Esher for her futile advice on the subject of husband keeping. "You must make the teakettle exciting," she said, meaning that a good woman must make ordinary life exciting if she hoped to keep her husband. Little did she suspect for whom his noble pot boiled. Such was the Victorian tradition—anything was acceptable except scandal.

Turn onto Pall Mall and follow it eastward from the St. James's Palace compound.

Pall Mall

This famous street, named for the seventeenth-century French version of croquet (*pallemaille*) first played along its tree-lined avenue, later became the site of a row of imposing gentlemen's clubs of truly palatial dimensions. Buildings on the opposite side of the street provided small establishments for bachelors or living quarters for politicians while they were meeting in the city. Exclusive shops occupied some of the ground floors.

Pall Mall with its imposing stone houses and men's clubs.

14. Red Lion Pub
Crown Passage

When a few yards east of St. James's Street, turn into Crown Passage, a narrow seventeenth-century street with tiny shops. If you are ready for lunch, the popular Red Lion Pub here is the second oldest pub on London's west side. An excellent, typical pub lunch, featuring steak and kidney pie, salads, and "ploughmans" (the hearty bread, cheese, pickled onion and chutney combinations which are to England what the hamburger is to America), is served in the upstairs lounge.

Crown Passage leads to King Street's antique shops and art galleries. Christie's International Auction House at number 8, founded in 1766, was a favorite haunt of Wilde's, especially when he was in the nearby St. James's Theatre every day in February of 1892 for rehearsals of *Lady Windermere's Fan* (which he wrote with Lillie Langtry in mind).

15. Site of the St. James's Theatre
Golden Lion Pub
King Street

Although his novel *The Portrait of Dorian Gray* had been hugely successful, *Lady Windermere's Fan* was Wilde's first major success as a playwright. When he took his curtain call after its opening in the St. James's Theatre, he complimented the enthusiastic audience upon its good taste and intelligence in appreciating his play! A few years later, when *The*

St. James's Theatre as it looked in the nineteenth century when it was the site of Wilde's first theatrical successes.

Importance of Being Earnest opened at the same theatre and the audience roared its applause and demanded an appearance by the playwright, Wilde amused them by announcing from his box, "Mr. Wilde is not here tonight." Later in the greenroom the Prince of Wales complimented the play by advising him not to cut a word of it.

The St. James's Theatre was torn down in 1957 in spite of a strong protest movement led by Laurence Olivier and Vivien Leigh. The Golden Lion Pub, with its elaborate sign, still stands adjacent to the old theatre site, and retains the aura of Victorian glamor that once permeated it when stars, writers, actors and managers stopped in for a relaxing drink.

Now you might like to wend your way eastward along King Street for a block or two, weaving in and out of the little side streets filled with antique shops and fine art galleries that run off to the right and left. Then return back through Crown Passage to Pall Mall and continue walking east.

16. Residence of Benjamin Disraeli
15 Pall Mall

At age twenty-seven, with a mite of literary recognition under his belt, Disraeli left his family home in Bloomsbury to take a flat in Pall Mall, which he considered the "right" part of town in which to pursue a political career. To his chagrin his application for membership was rejected by both the exclusive Athenaeum and Travellers clubs across the street. His only recourse, it seemed, was to acquire more powerful friends. Thus he set in motion a strategy of social climbing that probably has never been surpassed.

Impressed by her address on King Street, he first wooed and won Clara Bolton, the exquisite wife of a physician who used her as a decoy to attract wealthy patients. The affair with Clara, however, only lasted until "Dizzy," as his friends called him, acquired social contacts more important to his career. As his social skills improved, he began to cut quite a figure with his black ringlets, black velvet suit lined with white satin, and elaborately embroidered waistcoats. Across his breast sparkled a mass of gold chains. Rings adorned his fingers, and attached to his wrist by a tasseled cord hung a cane. Women loved him.

As he wormed his way into the political arena, he improved his living arrangement by moving a short distance away to 35 Duke Street. Meanwhile he had acquired a political sponsor, Sir Francis Sykes, as well as a new inamorata, Sir Francis's wife, Henrietta Sykes. This gentleman's health conveniently dictated long sessions at spas on the Continent, leaving Henrietta free to visit Dizzy's rooms, where she reveled in being "snugly placed by him on the comfortable couch, sipping coffee and kisses at the same time."

All did not remain calm in paradise, unfortunately. Clara Bolton, his former paramour on King Street, became aware of what was going on on Duke Street and didn't like it. She turned her considerable charm upon her rival's husband, Sir Francis, when he returned from his sojourn at the spa and managed to poison his mind against his political protégé, Dizzy. In the process, steeped in resentment toward her former lover, Clara succumbed to Sir Francis's retaliatory action and became his mistress.

Following a series of bitter accusations and counteraccusations which could have ruined Dizzy's career almost before it had gotten started, Henrietta had the good fortune to arrive home early one afternoon and surprise her errant husband in bed with Clara. To avert scandal, they came to an agreement. Henrietta would cover for her husband and his mistress Clara so long as he didn't make trouble for Dizzy. To seal the pact, Henrietta cheerfully accompanied Clara and Sir Francis on a "goodwill" trip to Paris, while Dizzy moved to 31A Park Street in Mayfair to be nearer to Henrietta, who was still living with her husband at 34 Upper Grosvenor.

At age thirty-five, Dizzy finally married and settled down with a rich widow ten years his senior. His political career soared. He served two separate terms as prime minister under Queen Victoria, who adored him, and he made enough money on his last novel, *Endymion,* to buy a seven-year lease on a mansion in Mayfair when he retired after being defeated in the 1880 election. Above all Disraeli ended up as Earl of Beaconsfield, a title well earned.

17. 48 Pall Mall

In 1874 Jimmy Whistler organized a show of his own work in a gallery at this location to spite a Royal Academy show that had opened with nothing of his included. Too far ahead of its time, his exhibition of thirteen paintings and fifty prints was not a huge success. A public that preferred "foolish sunsets to the poetry of the night" was not yet ready for his stark portraits and the little arrangements he called "symphonies."

18. Site of the Marlborough Club
52 Pall Mall

A few buildings away, at number 52, the Prince of Wales founded the elite Marlborough Club in defiance of the policy committee at White's, which refused to allow smoking in the morning room. Here his friends were permitted to smoke, drink, gamble and dine whenever or wherever they wished. The club eventually disbanded. The clubs lining the south side of Pall Mall, however, remain as active and exclusive today as they were in the nineteenth century. Among them are:

19. Reform Club
105 Pall Mall

The elegant Reform Club is a home of liberalism and a favorite among writers. It was here that Jules Verne's Phineas Fogg made the wager that he could go around the world in eighty days. It was also here that the uninhibited expatriate American, Jimmy Whistler, when he was introduced as a potential member, erupted with his raucous peacock laugh and awakened a lustily snoring gentleman who was snoozing over his paper in the reading room. "No gentleman laughs like that," the old gentleman grumbled. Needless to say, Whistler was disqualified.

20. Travellers Club
106 Pall Mall

Standing side by side with the Reform Club in an identical Italianate building is the Travellers Club, which was founded in 1819 for those who had taken the "grand tour." A prerequisite for a proposed member required that he should have traveled a minimum of five hundred miles outside the British Isles in a straight line from London. (Today it is a thousand miles.) Distance was less important than personality, however. The Prince of Wales resigned when a member insisted upon blackballing Cecil Rhodes, whose African exploits the prince greatly admired.

21. Athenaeum Club
107 Pall Mall

On the corner of Pall Mall and Waterloo Place is the home of the prestigious Athenaeum Club, built on the site of the prince regent's Carlton House. Its first-floor drawing room is considered one of the grandest in London. Always known for its distinguished members, the club is favored by the hierarchy of the Anglican church, as well as by prominent men in science, art and literature. Disraeli did much of his writing in its rooms, but not at the beginning of his career when his application for membership was turned down.

Another prominent member was Sir James Barrie. On his first visit he asked an octogenarian biologist the way to the dining room. The biologist burst into tears. He had been a member of the club for fifty years. No one had ever spoken to him before.

Turn off Pall Mall to the north into St. James's Square.

22. St. James's Square

Dating from 1673, St. James's was the West End's first square, built by Henry Jermyn on land presented by Charles II. The equestrian statue replete with a molehill, shaded by lovely plane trees in the center of the square, depicts William III. It was the molehill over which the king's horse stumbled at Hampton Court in 1702 that caused the injury that brought about his death. Most of the buildings you see are nineteenth century, with the exception of some Georgian town houses on the north and west sides of the square and a few modern offices.

Chatham House, numbers 9 and 10 on the square, was occupied at various times by three prime ministers—William Ewart Gladstone (briefly), William Pitt the Elder and Lord Derby.

23. Residence of Waldorf Astor
4 St. James's Square

This aristocratic brick mansion, with its white columns, large ballroom and two dining rooms big enough to seat forty guests each, was once a social center hosted by the great-great-grandson of the American, John Jacob Astor, who made a fortune in fur trading.

When young Waldorf Astor's heart showed signs of strain (1908) and he was forced to give up polo, his father suggested he take over the *Pall Mall Gazette* for something to do. But even office work was too stressful, so as a last resort he opted for a political career. With Waldorf Astor in politics, a town house became a necessity, and at that time St. James's Square was one of the finest addresses in the city, which prompted the Astors' move here.

Nancy Astor, his American wife, took a lively interest in his new endeavor. All London was astonished that this rich society hostess could rough it in the slums as she canvassed door to door to get votes. Had it not been for the experience she gained then, she would not have been the first woman to get into Parliament when her husband succeeded to the peerage in 1919, and she was elected to his old seat of Plymouth.

As you walk around the square, you will pass King Street on its west side. Exit here after you finish browsing.

24. Residence of Napoleon III
8 King Street

Louis Napoleon lived here in exile after the fall of his uncle, Emperor Napoleon Bonaparte, and prior to becoming president of the Second Republic in 1848 and later proclaiming himself emperor of France. In London he busied himself by collecting books and family portraits and dabbling in real estate. He owned several houses, occupying another one nearby at number One Carlton Gardens from 1840 to 1841 and maintaining a third on Berkeley Street, which he purchased for a Miss Howard, who later in Paris was endowed with the title of Comtesse de Beauregard.

Now return through St. James's Square and cross Pall Mall into Carlton House Terrace. Continue east on Carlton House Terrace. On the way you will pass Waterloo Place on the left.

25. Residence of Lord Curzon, Viceroy to India
1 Carlton House Terrace

Among the concentration of monuments on Waterloo Place is one to the statesman Lord Curzon. Historically referred to as "a very superior person," he once bragged that, upon discovering a housemaid who had allowed a footman to spend the night with her, he "put the little slut out into the street at a moment's notice"—this from a gentleman whose affair with Lady Ribbesdale (whose widower later escorted Rosa Lewis, the proprietress of the nearby Cavendish Hotel) was hardly a secret, and who later became the enamored escort of novelist Elinor Glyn after she wrote about a Balkan queen clad in diaphanous garments, who received her lover while lying on a tiger skin.

Later, when Lloyd George was prime minister and "the superior person" was still foreign secretary, a colleague said to Lloyd George, "If you treated me half as badly as you treat Curzon, I'd resign tomorrow morning."

"Oh, he does resign," replied George. "But there are two messengers at the Foreign Office. One has a limp; he comes with the resignation. The other was a champion runner; he always catches him up."

26. Residence of William Waldorf Astor
18 Carlton House Terrace

This first American Astor to take English citizenship arrived in 1890 with a fortune inherited from his father, John Jacob II. He had hoped that his son would marry into the English peerage, so Waldorf's choice of the American Nancy Shaw was a disappointment, compounded by the fact that she was a divorcée. After he had met her, however, he said, "If she is good enough for you, Waldorf, she will be good enough for me."

His generosity was greatly appreciated in London. He built and endowed the Children's Clinic at Great Ormond Street Hospital.

27. Residence of William Ewart Gladstone
22 Carlton House Terrace

William Gladstone may have been Lillie Langtry's dear friend, but Queen Victoria vowed that she'd rather abdicate than see "that half-mad firebrand" oust her favored Disraeli as prime minister. Nevertheless a general election in 1880 voted out the Tories, and the Liberal Gladstone came into power. Victoria, of course, didn't abdicate, much to the disappointment of the Prince of Wales. Instead she delayed making the appointment official for weeks, until Bertie, influenced by Lillie, sent a note to his mother suggesting that it would be far better to take the initiative than have it forced upon her.

The queen was shocked at his impertinence. Having condemned the prince since boyhood as a poor reflection of his late father, she had refused him even the most insignificant role in governing. Until now, however, she hadn't had to contend with the lovely Lillie. When Lillie had inadvertently learned that Gladstone held a high regard for the prince's potential in foreign relations, especially with France, she had urged Bertie to risk the note, hoping Gladstone's rising influence might provide an opportunity for the prince to prove himself.

As it turned out, the note did more to enhance Lillie's influence than the prince's. When in her own time Victoria at last sent for Gladstone, the imprudent old man fancied an indebtedness to the prince's paramour. He encouraged Lillie to use his name as a social credential and after her fall from favor, saw to it that nobody in society snubbed her. The kindly old man also permitted Oscar Wilde to use his name when Wilde was attempting to get his early poems published in *The Spectator.*

Gladstone was intensely religious and, unlike his neighbor Curzon, dedicated many a night to roaming London's dark alleys giving money to prostitutes and trying to reform them. On more than one occasion, he even brought one home to shelter.

Mrs. Gladstone often hosted church socials in their home. One time a guest launched into a spirited argument over an interpretation of a biblical passage. Aware of Mrs. Gladstone's apparent discomfort as the discussion grew heated, one of the party tried to put a stop to it by remarking piously, "Well, there is One above who knows all things."

Mrs. Gladstone's face brightened. "Yes," she said, "and Mr. Gladstone will be coming down in a few minutes."

Serious as he appeared, the grand old man did have a sense of humor. He once admired a seventeenth-century oil painting in an antique shop, which depicted an aristocrat dressed in an old Spanish costume with a ruff, plumed hat and lace cuffs. He wanted it badly, but thought the price too high. Sometime later at the house of a rich London merchant, he came upon the portrait. His host, noticing Gladstone's admiration, approached him. "You like it?" he asked. "It's a portrait of one of my ancestors, a minister at the court of Queen Elizabeth."

"Three pounds less and he would have been *my* ancestor," Gladstone retorted.

When Gladstone resigned his office as prime minister, he reluctantly sold his prized collection of china and Wedgwood along with the Carlton Terrace house. "I had grown to the house," he wrote, "having lived more time in it than in any other since I was born, and mainly by reason of all that was done in it."

Another neighbor on Carlton House Terrace was Lord St. George Lonsdale, a rake whose turf winnings barely outstripped his boudoir accomplishments. While his pleasure-loving lady (who after his ignoble demise remarried and became Lady Ripon) was in the south of France, Lord Lonsdale suddenly took ill, *not* in his usual London abode, but found himself dying in a house he maintained to wine and dine freewheeling actresses. For the sake of respectability, his dead body was smuggled, sitting upright, in a cab from 30 Bryanston Street to the Lonsdale mansion on Carlton House Terrace, where it could be put to rest "discreetly."

Walk back to Waterloo Place and turn down the few steps leading south to the pink-surfaced Mall, the royal processional road that leads to Buckingham Palace.

28. St. James's Park

As you walk along the Mall, St. James's Park with its lake is on your left. It is the oldest of London's royal parks and was created, like the others, by Henry VIII from land seized from Westminster Abbey. In 1829 the great architect John Nash redesigned it, creating the lake and giving it the appearance it has now. At night it is particularly romantic, with its illuminated fountains and the flood-lit Buckingham Palace beyond.

29. Marlborough House
The Mall

Before reaching the Queen Victoria Memorial, you will pass Marlborough House on your right, to which the Prince of Wales brought his bride of the fast-turning cartwheels. Built by Christopher Wren in 1709-1710 for Sarah, Duchess of Marlborough, and later enlarged for Prince Leopold until he became Leopold I of the Belgians, it awaited the marriage and subsequent occupancy of the Prince of Wales in 1863 to become the liveliest spot in town.

As Princess Alexandra relied more and more upon an ear trumpet, her enjoyment of social life waned, and eventually mothering took precedence over partying. Thus the prince, in his lusty midtwenties, lost interest in his beautiful, delicate wife.

The strictest of codes existed between them, however. No scandal would be allowed to embarrass her. On state occasions and at Marlborough's coveted garden parties, she appeared at his side, even after Lillie Langtry came into his life. They were utterly discreet. Perhaps Alexandra simply closed her eyes to Lillie; or perhaps she felt relieved that the prince had settled down to a single paramour. Whatever the case, Lillie was accepted at Marlborough House functions

A Garden Party at Marlborough House as depicted in the Pictorial World *of August 4, 1883. The Prince of Wales is in the top hat on the left, Alexandra on the right, and Lillie Langtry displays her elaborate bustle.*

when Alexandra was present, and later, during Lillie's career as an actress, Alexandra attended most of her London openings with the Prince of Wales.

Although the Prince of Wales accepted Oscar Wilde as Lillie's confidante, and they frequently met at social functions in the houses of other aristocrats, the elegantly attired prince did not always approve of Wilde's showy costumes. Wilde was not numbered among the exclusive "Marlborough Set."

30. Buckingham Palace
The Mall

The end of the Mall is dominated by the Queen Victoria Memorial in the front of Buckingham Palace, originally built for the Duke of Buckingham in 1703. Since Victoria's accession in 1837, it has been the residence of the royal family.

Tragic as was Victoria's loss of her beloved Prince Consort Albert, and as reputably austere as were social occasions in her palace, she still enjoyed infrequent moments of mirth. In order to hear how the HMS *Eurydice,* a frigate sunk off Portsmouth, had been salvaged, the queen invited Admiral Foley to lunch. Having exhausted this melancholy subject, the queen then inquired after her close friend, the admiral's sister. Hard of hearing, the admiral replied in a stentorial voice, "Well, ma'am, I am going to have her turned over, take a good look at her bottom and have it well scraped." The queen put down her knife and fork, hid her face in her handkerchief, and laughed until the tears ran down her cheeks.

The good queen died at Osborne House on the Isle of Wight on January 22, 1901. As she lay on her deathbed, a member of the royal household conversing with her son, about to become King Edward VII, mused, "I wonder if she will be happy in heaven?"

"I don't know," said the prince. "She will have to walk *behind* the angels—and she won't like that."

The coronation procession of King Edward VII in June of 1901.

On the day in June set for the Prince of Wales's coronation, throngs lined the streets, flags waved and bands played all in vain. Suddenly the crowd stilled. Word spread that the prince was ill. He had appendicitis. Thus the coronation ceremony was postponed. Two months later in the heat of August, once again flags went up, crowds gathered and the famous eight cream-colored horses appeared, drawing the antique golden coach with its crystal panels through which, this time, could be seen the king and the queen. Popular enthusiasm knew no bounds. The roar of continuous cheering echoed from the palace to Westminster.

"The three women I have most admired," Oscar Wilde said a year before his death, "are Queen Victoria, Sarah Bernhardt and Lillie Langtry. I would have married any one of them with pleasure. The first had great dignity, the second a lovely voice, the third a perfect figure."

Although Wilde never made it to Marlborough House, his wife Constance was presented to the queen in 1887. At that time Constance, inspired by Oscar, was busy giving talks advocating a departure from French fashion in favor of looser, lighter clothing. For her presentation, however, she donned an exact copy of the fashion at the time when Victoria had ascended the throne.

Lillie Langtry had been presented earlier, in 1879, at one of Victoria's Buckingham Palace "afternoon drawing rooms." For her presentation she wore a gown of ivory brocade with a long court train, lined with the same pale yellow as the Marechal Neil roses she carried (a gift from the prince), hanging from her shoulders. Atop her head were three huge ostrich plumes, reminiscent of the prince's crest.

When the sovereign is in residence, the royal standard flies over the palace night and day. On state occasions the sovereign appears with members of the royal family on the central balcony.

A visit to the palace should be timed to coincide with the changing of the guard, which occurs daily at 11:30 A.M. Also worth a visit is the Queen's Gallery, where there are various displays of items from the royal art collection.

Now retrace your steps along the Mall to the Queen's Walk, where you can turn left and continue north alongside Green Park to Piccadilly.

31. Piccadilly

Turn right toward Piccadilly Circus where you began, stopping for tea in the refined Palm Court of the Ritz Hotel if you are appropriately dressed (jackets and ties for men).

Further along Piccadilly you will surely want to stop at Fortnum & Masons for lunch or tea if you missed the Ritz. This is the grocery store of the royal family, and certainly Wilde must have stopped here on his perambulations down Piccadilly. It is world famous for its morning-coated assistants and the great clock over the door where, on the hour, figures of Mr. Fortnum and Mr. Mason emerge to the tune of the "Eton Boating Song." The store was established in 1707 by Mason, a grocer, and Fortnum, one of Queen Anne's footmen. It is now beautifully stocked with delicatessen food and gourmet items, and also has a tearoom.

At number 187 is another haunt of Wilde's, Hatchard's bookshop, established in 1797. This and Fortnum & Masons are the sole remaining shops of this once-thriving eighteenth-century shopping area. When Wilde was released from prison and preparing for his self-inflicted exile to France, the only appearance he made in public was a stop at Hatchard's to stock up on books. Even though his weight had dropped from 190 to 168 pounds and two years of confinement had taken the edge from his buoyant personality, the bookseller recognized him and greeted him with affection.

When you arrive back at Eros on Piccadilly Circus where you began, you have finished the St. James's walk. Next we'll explore Mayfair.

WALK

MAYFAIR

THREE

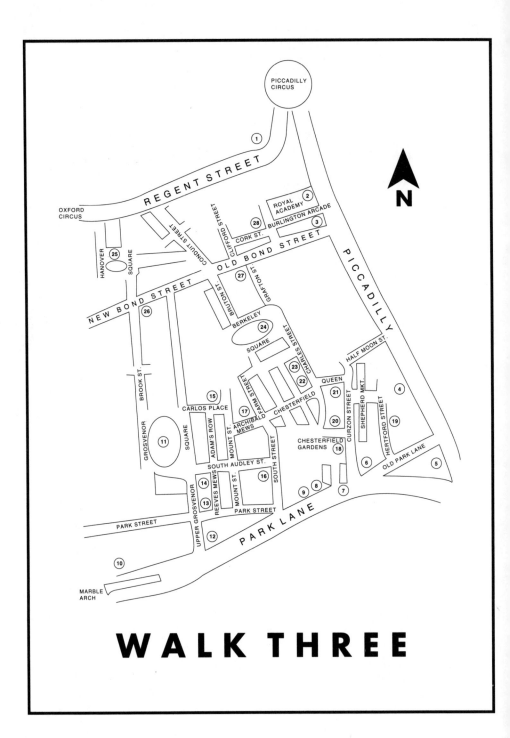

WALK THREE

Broadly speaking, thé boundaries of Mayfair are drawn by Regent Street, Oxford Street, Park Lane and Piccadilly. Although nightingales no longer sing in Berkeley Square, and Mayfair is not quite so fashionable as it was when a team of zebras pulled Alfred Rothschild's carriage along Piccadilly, it still is charged with an ambience of extravagant luxury for those who know where to look. As a prominent London television news analyst advised us, one must look "up" to see what made London beautiful.

"Look up, and look back," we say. What remains of the Piccadilly and Park Lane grand mansions is now covered by the false fronts of shops at ground level. You must "distance yourself" on the opposite side of the street to glimpse their upper-story grandeur, just as you must look back a hundred years to imagine the glitter of lives lived within their heavy stone walls.

Originally the May Fair was an annual event that took place in an open area between Berkeley Street and Park Lane. In George III's time it was suppressed because it created a public nuisance, the area around Shepherd Market being especially deplorable. Then the aristocrats arrived. First came the town houses of the landed gentry, a few of whom still maintain residences here. Next came the hotels for aristocrats who didn't live in town. Most of the town houses are gone or have been divided into elegant flats, but the hotels remain.

Piccadilly Circus

We begin on the north side of Piccadilly Circus. Walk a short distance to tiny Air Street, which cuts through to the front of the Café Royal.

1. Café Royal
68 Regent Street

This distinguished restaurant has been frequented by celebrities since it opened in 1865. Its Domino Room was a regular meeting place for Whistler, Aubrey Beardsley, Max Beerbohm, Frank Harris, Walter Sickert and other luminaries of the 1890s, but most especially for Wilde and Whistler during the productive years of their friendship. The two made a striking pair— little, dapper Whistler with his shock of curly black hair interrupted by the celebrated white lock he called his *mèche de Silas* (often mistaken for a floating feather), his tuft of a mustache, and his monocle in one eye, and tall, portly Wilde, fancied up in a bronze-colored suit with its back custom tailored to resemble the outline of a cello, and a sunflower smiling from his lapel.

Whistler was impressed with the "N" engraved on the Café Royal's wineglasses, which were supposed to have come from the Tuileries in 1870, but no matter how many were broken, more appeared. He also loved the menu, especially the *poulet en casserole,* accompanied with a wonderful *Coute Mallard* wine which he had discovered there. While the wine flowed, he and Wilde would argue ceaselessly about art. Neither one let his mind dwell on politics, theology or science. (Wilde said: "There is hardly a person in the House of Commons worth painting, though many of them would be better for a little whitewashing.")

Both fancied themselves apostles of beauty. Whistler, twenty years older, experienced, and with a wit equal to Wilde's, was irresistible to the new graduate in search of a prophet, while Whistler, for his part, was flattered by homage from the young Wilde, whose name was on everyman's tongue as the most promising poet and man of letters of his generation. Moreover, whose companionship could be more amusing? Or stimulating?

While they agreed over the relative importance of art, they disagreed as to what comprised art. To Whistler there was only one art—painting. Wilde placed literature before all other arts and resented that in England only painters were referred to as "artists," while others were called by the art they practiced—musicians and writers.

There was no homosexual attachment between the two; it was strictly a relationship of the intellect, while it lasted. But inevitably it proved of short duration: two oversized egos in competition. After one of Whistler's brilliant sallies, Wilde said, "I wish that I had said that, Whistler."

"You will, Oscar, you will," Whistler answered. As the friendship cooled, he accused Wilde of poaching his every remark and of preaching doctrines in his lectures which Whistler had expounded for years, an accusation Wilde could never deny. "It is only the unimaginative who ever invents," Wilde said. "The true artist is known by the use he makes of what he annexes, and he annexes everything." Whistler, on the other hand, was too vain to realize that his own theories of art had been adopted largely from Gautier.

As Wilde began to learn that his nature was incompatible with the bonds of domestic life, his tall, bulky figure, bundled in his famous astrakhan-collared green coat, was seen more often than not lounging and smoking at a corner table in the Café Royal, where he lamented to confidantes, "The only way a woman can possibly reform a man is by boring him so completely that he loses all interest in life." Since he was not about to lose interest in life, the Café Royal became Wilde's escape from boredom.

Another habitué, who often dined with Wilde, was Aubrey Beardsley, labeled as a "decadent" in the context of nineteenth-century artists revolting against the harsh sexual repression of the Victorian Age. An English parallel to Henri de Toulouse-Lautrec's scenes of Parisian nightlife, Beardsley's daring drawings, designed as covers for the scandalous *The Yellow Book,* depicted sensual women from history and myth, along with actresses, dancers or prostitutes from the theatres and cafés of London's West End. Among his finest drawings are a study of a group of waiters at the Café Royal, and another titled *The Fat Woman,* that shows a demimondaine sitting at a café table.

Wilde admired the young Beardsley and went far in promoting his career, even assigning him the commission to illustrate his play *Salomé* for publication in 1893. The drawings turned out to be more controversial in their sexuality than the play, and the resulting notoriety prompted Whistler and publisher John Lane, in the process of conceiving *The Yellow Book* as a vehicle for avant-garde literature, to appoint Beardsley its first art director. Perhaps because of Whistler's association with the magazine, a resentful Wilde was not invited to join its coterie of writers, among whom were the American Henry James, Max Beerbohm and Edmund Gosse. Wilde predicted a short life for the quarterly. He was right.

2. The Royal Academy of Arts
Piccadilly

Walk back to Piccadilly and proceed a short distance west to the imposing Royal Academy of Arts, formerly Burlington House. Its prestigious annual summer exhibition has focused since the eighteenth century upon contemporary works not yet exhibited. Through the years there have been bitter altercations about the choice of work selected for this show, and also the places where paintings are hung. Whistler finally had a painting accepted by the Royal Academy in 1863, a portrait called *At the Piano,* which engendered mild recognition, but not enough to counteract the ridicule occasioned by his more abstract canvasses that followed.

Burlington House, home of the Royal Academy of Arts.

An invitation to attend the private viewing of the annual exhibition and the Academy soirée that followed was as highly coveted by society as an invitation to show his work was by an artist.

After returning from his first American tour in 1883, Wilde found himself low on funds, so he was pleased to accept a local lecture contract, one that included a talk he titled "The House Beautiful," to be presented at the Royal Academy's art school. Whistler was consumed with jealousy that the Royal Academy should consider Wilde authoritative on art. The lecture was a huge success, nevertheless, and Wilde repeated it on a tour throughout the British Isles.

Private View of the Old Master Exhibition 1888 of the
Royal Academy of Arts, *painted by H.J. Brooks in 1889.*
J.E. Millais, Holman Hunt, and John Ruskin are among
those pictured, (courtesy of the National Portrait
Gallery, London).

It was while on this tour in Dublin that Wilde became
engaged to Constance Lloyd. He had met her several years
earlier through a friend of his mother's. They were
immediately attracted to each other, but his American tour
had intervened. In describing his fiancée to friends, Wilde
said that "she could draw music from the piano so sweet that
the birds stop singing to listen to her."

3. Burlington Arcade
Piccadilly

This covered shopping street is as pleasant (and
expensive) today as it was in 1819 when built by Lord George
Cavendish. Its thirty-eight shops are protected by top-hatted
beadles (security men) dedicated to seeing that patrons
adhere to rules established in the nineteenth century, which
outlaw whistling, hurrying or singing within the confines of
the arcade.

4. Rothschild Row
Piccadilly

At the time Wilde was enchanting nineteenth-century hostesses with poetry and *bon mots,* the western end of Piccadilly was commonly known as Rothschild Row. "All that one should know about modern life is where the Duchesses are; anywhere else is quite demoralizing," says Wilde's protagonist in *An Ideal Husband.* Well, Mayfair is where the duchesses were in his time, so it might be amusing to pause in another of our favorite pubs, the Rose and Crown, around the corner from where Piccadilly meets Park Lane, and ruminate a bit upon the former aristocracy of Rothschild Row.

During the latter part of the nineteenth century, this international banking family was so rich and powerful that not only did it dominate Mayfair, it controlled the financial balance of all Europe. The London branch of the family, like the Vienna, Naples and Paris branches, made countless contributions to mankind, subsidized more art dealers than anyone in Europe, and championed more causes.

Sir Nathan Meyer Rothschild was the first Rothschild to settle in London. Like his brothers spread around Europe, Nathan was more interested in making money than in spending it. After a concert in his home at 107 Piccadilly presented by Louis Spohr, he congratulated the well-known composer, then jingled some coins in his pocket. "*That's* my music," he said.

By 1865 Sir Nathan's "music" had earned him a knighthood. Until 1885 he was a member of Parliament, and later became the first Jew to be admitted to the House of Lords.

But he never forgot the long climb upward. Alighting from a hansom cab one evening, he gave the driver what he felt to be an adequate tip. "Your lordship's son always gives me a good deal more than this," said the driver.

"I daresay he does," responded Nathan, "but then, you see, he has a rich father. I haven't."

Nathan and his wife Hannah had seven children. Most of them or their descendants lived in the grand houses of Rothschild Row. Lionel, Nathan's son and heir, built number 148, adjacent to Wellington's Apsley House, which his son Nattie later inherited. Mayer, Lionel's brother, moved into number 107 after Nathan's death and left it to his only child, Hannah Rothschild Rosebery. Louise, the widow of Lionel's brother Anthony, lived a golden sovereign's toss away at 19 Grosvenor Gate. Alfred, the most extravagant of Lionel's sons, built his ostentatious mansion nearby at One Seamore Place. Leo, his sporting brother who married a relative of the rich Sassoon family, lived barely off Piccadilly at 5 Hamilton Place. And then two Rothschilds from the Austrian branch of the family, who had emigrated to London, Ferdinand and his sister Alice, lived at numbers 143 and 142 Piccadilly, respectively. No wonder it was called Rothschild Row!

Not all of these palatial establishments still stand, but it is worth a pause to imagine the extravagant scenarios that were such an integral part of London's "romantic nineties." Considered the most imposing was 148 Piccadilly, built by Baron Lionel Rothschild, head of the London Bank. Elegantly clad ladies in tiaras and their escorts in swallowtailed coats ascended an imposing marble staircase leading up to a gilt-and-scarlet ballroom on the first floor, where they sipped champagne and looked out into the night from huge windows hung with silk-embroidered river goddesses. A silver table service by Garrard, weighing nearly 650 pounds, enhanced a table set with apple green Sevres china painted by Le Bel. Every chair, a wit remarked, offered gilt-edged security. Queen Victoria refused a request from Gladstone to grant a peerage to Lionel Rothschild because she believed that "one who owed his wealth to loans with foreign governments or successful speculation on the stock exchange" didn't deserve the honor, but society never refused an invitation to Baron Lionel's fêtes. (Victorian maxim: "The best people spend money, but do not earn it.")

Lionel's sons were the third generation of Rothschilds to live in England, but the first to have an education. Natty, the eldest, attended the university with the Prince of Wales while the latter was doing his stint at Trinity College, Cambridge. Through Natty the prince became friendly with all of the Rothschilds, in Paris and elsewhere, and they rewarded the prince's patronage with help for his finances, which were mighty dicey at times. Unlike his mother, the prince found the new breed of millionaire far more amusing than the landed gentry. When the prince became King Edward VII, Natty was the first Rothschild to be made a lord.

Ferdinand Rothschild, from the Austrian branch of the family, became an English citizen and acquired 143 Piccadilly.

An intellectual with fine taste in art, he once gave a ball to honor Crown Prince Rudolph of Austria, with the Prince of Wales present. To make his ball especially enchanting, he offered to present gowns to twelve of the most beautiful guests, Lillie Langtry among them. Lillie included a petticoat with hers and later received a bill from the designer. Ferdie had authorized payment for the gown, but not the petticoat to go with it.

Ferdie Rothschild may have been the intellectual giant of his generation, but Alfred had the most fun. He was also the most extravagant Rothschild. (He was so used to the luxury of hothouse-grown strawberries that he once inveighed against March because it was the end of the strawberry season.) On his grounds at One Seamore Place, he kept a pet goat that was permitted to roam Piccadilly at will. Because Lord Lionel, his father, had made it known that a policeman would never go hungry if he called at 148 Piccadilly, which many on night watch did, Rothschild carriages, with their dark blue hoods and the thin yellow stripe around their bodies, were always allowed the right-of-way on local streets—along with Alfred's goat. Drivers' surprise at sidestepping a goat on city streets, however, was nothing compared to their astonishment at the sight of Alfred racing along Piccadilly in his carriage, pulled by a team of striped zebras.

Lady Warwick wrote in her memoirs that she had heard the greatest artists in the world—Adelina Patti, Nellie Melba, Franz Liszt, and Jean de Reszke—all perform in Alfred's white drawing room, conducted by Alfred himself with his diamond-studded ivory baton. At other times he assembled ponies, dogs and hoops to create his own circus with himself as ringmaster, adorned in a blue frock coat and lavender kid gloves, and cracking a long whip.

He used, also, to hold intimate little gatherings called "adoration" dinners by inviting one particularly alluring lady to dine with him and three or four other gentlemen, and then giving a gift to the lady. Lillie Langtry was so honored. At the end of the evening, Alfred drew her aside. "What shall I give you, beautiful lady?"

Lillie promptly picked up a lavishly bejeweled Louis XVI snuffbox. "This will do," she replied. Afterward she wrote in her journal that for a moment she had thought he would have a heart attack, but when he got his breath, he promised her something "much prettier," and out came one of his well-known gift boxes.

Of the stories told about Alfred's hospitality, one of the most amusing concerned the time when a guest asked for milk in his tea, and the powdered flunky asked, "Jersey, Hereford or Shorthorn, sir?"

The one fear that haunted old Nathan was that his beautiful daughter Hannah might be tempted to marry outside the faith. As a safeguard, just before dying he added a clause to his will stating that his daughters would be disinherited if they married without the consent of their mother or brothers. When Hannah announced to her recently widowed mother that she was determined to marry tall, attractive Henry Fitzroy, brother of the Earl of Southampton and a prospective member of Parliament, terrible scenes ensued. He was not a Jew. Only her soft-hearted brother Nathaniel finally relented. The rest of the Rothschilds were so incensed that none would attend her quiet wedding at St. George's on Hanover Square, and they never forgave her for abandoning her faith. When her young son died after a fall from his pony, her cousins interpreted it as a "punishment of God."

After World War I the English branch of the family was the hardest hit financially. The inheritance taxes of the three magnificent sons of Lionel, who all died within a two-year period, reduced the firm down to its last millions. Rothschild tradition ignored the females of the family in bequests, allowing their fortunes to pass unchallenged to Rothschild males, which accounts for so many Rothschilds marrying cousins. Alfred, however, defied tradition. When his will was read in 1917, the bulk of his estate, larger than Natty's or Leo's because of his bachelorhood, was left to his natural daughter, Almina Wombwell, wife of the Earl of Carnarvon.

Of the grand houses only 5 Hamilton Place remains, off Piccadilly to the right just before you reach Hyde Park Corner. It is now Les Ambassadeurs Club. Alfred's One Seamore Place was razed to give Curzon Street an outlet to Park Lane, and 148 Piccadilly, once neighbor to Apsley House, was razed to make another entrance into Hyde Park.

5. Apsley House—Residence of the Duke of Wellington
Hyde Park Corner

Apsley House marks Hyde Park Corner, Mayfair's western limit. Now the Wellington Museum, it was built in the 1770s by Robert Adam and extended in 1820 by the Iron Duke who defeated Napoleon at Waterloo. Wellington lived in it until his death in 1852. It is furnished with the heavy, ornate furniture of his time—more impressive than beautiful. Wilde had about as much admiration for warriors like the Duke of Wellington as he had for heavy furniture. "As long as war is regarded as wicked, it will always have its fascination. When it is looked upon as vulgar, it will cease to be popular," he wrote in his *Intentions*.

Continue north from the Rose and Crown Pub, the only pub on Park Lane. (Tradition warns us that patrons who stay here drinking too long hear a ghostly rattling of chains from its cellars, where prisoners of long ago awaited their turn at the Tyburn gallows.)

Park Lane, once synonymous with high living and sumptuous mansions, is now synonymous with luxury hotels. You can still steal a glimpse of the street's former grandeur, however, from two of the original nineteenth-century houses overlooking the park, numbers 93 and 99, both with delightful front bow windows and wrought-iron balconies.

6. Site of the Duke of Westminster's Residence
Park Lane (now the grosvenor House Hotel)

Oscar Wilde got off to a good start in London with an introduction to the Duchess of Westminster, the sister of his Oxford acquaintance, Ronald Gower. While walking through the lofty rooms of the Duke of Westminster's house, now the location of the Grosvenor House Hotel on Park Lane, he made a magnificent gesture and said to his fellow writer, Le Gallienne, "Ah, Richard! This is how a gentleman should live."

To be in society was, Wilde thought, a bore; but to be out of it was a tragedy. "To get into the best society now-a-days," he was heard to say, "one has either to feed people, amuse people, or shock people—that is all." As he could not afford to feed them, he amused and shocked them. Very quickly, however, he learned that that was not all that was needed. He discovered the importance of propitiating women like the Duchess of Westminster and Lillie Langtry in order to get on in the world. His amiable nature and delight in flattery, his interest in dress, and the strain of femininity in his boyishness made conversation with women as easy for them as talking to one of their own.

Park Lane. On this street, Oscar Wilde made his entrance into London Society.

An exciting interlude began at a ball given by Shelagh, Duchess of Westminster, in old Grosvenor House when the honored guest, the kaiser's son and crown prince, mysteriously disappeared during the party. Embarrassed equerries finally traced him to a bedroom, where he was taking a rest with a certain notorious peeress. The next day the appreciative Imperial Highness sent a magnificent jewel to the lady, not realizing it was one of the German crown jewels and not at his disposal. His furious father, the kaiser, called upon the German ambassador to demand the jewel be returned. The lady said no. Ambassadors on both sides grew grim during this "scandal of the season," but it was finally settled without the press finding out. The kaiser won, but only by offering a substantial substitute.

7. Residence of Benjamin and Mary Anne Disraeli
93 Park Lane

Benjamin Disraeli resided in this sumptuous corner house with its bays and balconies from after his marriage in 1839 until the death of his wife, Mary Anne Lewis, who owned it. Dizzy, as she called him, had been a political partner of her late husband, Wyndham Lewis, who had helped him get into Parliament. Mary Anne, forty-six years old when they married, admitted to being eight years Dizzy's senior, but was actually twelve years older. Although she realized that Dizzy had married her for the vast fortune she had inherited when her husband had dropped dead of a heart attack, the marriage brought him great contentment. She often said, "Dizzy married me for money, but if he were to marry me today, it would be for love." In her later years she appeared in public grotesquely made up and overdressed, attempting to appear younger, but Dizzy was always the gallant, treating her with respect and genuine affection.

After his wife died, Disraeli purchased a seven-year lease on a residence at 19 Curzon Street from Lord Tankerville, which he paid for with proceeds from his last novel, *Endymion*. He lived to be seventy-seven, wittily weathering his advancing age with remarks like: "When I meet a man whose name I can't remember, I give myself two minutes; then if it is hopeless, I say, 'And how is the old complaint?'"

8. Site of Edward Sassoon's Residence
Park Lane (now the London Hilton)

Edward Sassoon inherited a Kensington Gore house from his father, but had long concealed a distaste for the baroque establishment, so within a few months of Sir Albert's death, Edward and his wife Aline purchased an imposing mansion near Rothschild Row which overlooked Stanhope Gate, now the location of the Hilton Hotel. Its former owners, the unstable Rand millionaire Barney Barnato and his nervous wife, who had been swung aloft by a crane to cement photographs of themselves under the cornerstone, had relished a series of hideous figures on the roof which, according to the publisher Labouchere, were "creditors turned to stone while awaiting settlement"—the same creditors who were preempted by Barnato's suicide, no doubt.

It took Edward and Aline three years to undo Barnato's architectural crimes. They then graced the house with Lalique glass chandeliers and exquisite eighteenth-century furniture. The new baronet imported some rococo paneling from a palace in Venice and toured galleries all over Europe for suitable paintings.

Edward left the house to his son Philip, and many exhibitions benefiting hospitals and other charities were held there before it was demolished to make way for the London Hilton.

9. Dudley House
100 Park Lane

It was in this house, with its bow windows and lovely balcony (now enclosed) overlooking the park, that the Prince of Wales celebrated when his horse Persimmon won the Derby in June, 1896. His hostess, with whom he supped alone at midnight following a dinner at the Jockey Club, was Georgiana, Countess of Dudley. Lady Dudley, along with Lillie Langtry, was the lady most frequently referred to in various Victorian memoirs as the "most beautiful woman I ever saw." Crowds gathered on Rotten Row to watch her barouche pass by, in which she sat erect with the indifference of an Oriental, under a brown holland umbrella which she held over her elderly husband, one of the richest men in England. Although he was twenty years her senior and unfaithful to her, she adored him. When Georgiana, the daughter of Scottish Baronet Sir Thomas Moncreiffe, became Lord Dudley's second wife, her mother gave her one sage bit of advice: *never* comment on a likeness. Georgiana found it a tactful rule to follow while admiring Edwardian babies. Considering the "discreet" morality of the time, one could never be certain of the true identity of the fathers.

When Lord Dudley died at seventy, he left Georgiana a very rich young widow. She entertained lavishly in this house that still stands at the corner of Park Lane and Culross—so lavishly that she once had to sell her double strand of pearls for seventeen thousand pounds, which caused somewhat of a row when her son claimed that they were heirlooms.

10. Marble Arch
Park Lane

At the north end of Park Lane is the Marble Arch where, on the park side, Speaker's Corner is reserved for those with anything to say who wish to say it publicly. The arch once stood in the forecourt of Buckingham Palace, but was too narrow to permit carriages through, so it was brought to this spot in 1850, near the place where the public gallows known as Tyburn Tree had once stood.

Turn right on Oxford Street and walk to Park Street, then turn right again down to Upper Grosvenor. Turn left on Upper Grosvenor and follow it to Grosvenor Square.

The Marble Arch entrance to Hyde Park.

11. United States Embassy
Grosvenor Square

The Grosvenor family, who later became the Westminsters, still owns the freehold of most of the properties in the three-hundred-acre estate which encompasses Mayfair and Park Lane, including the site of the American Embassy, which dominates Grosvenor Square. Return to Upper Grosvenor and walk west.

12. Residence of Christopher Sykes
34 Upper Grosvenor

Along this attractive street lived several of the Prince of Wales's closest friends, among them the subservient Sykes, often the unfortunate butt of princely jokes. On the circuit of aristocratic country-house parties, Sykes's three-thousand-acre estate at Brantingthorpe frequently hosted the prince and his party. To rate the Royal as a house-party guest was a highly coveted privilege. More than one friend trying to "keep up" with the Rothschilds went into bankruptcy. The hapless Sykes was so unfailingly deferential that the prince often amused himself by pouring brandy over his head, which struck the prince's cortège as hilariously funny, almost as funny as the time the prince deposited a dead seagull in bed with the inebriated Sykes after a royal ball. Eventually the time came when poor Sykes was beggaring himself. To the prince's credit, when he realized his loyal friend's predicament, he arranged for richer friends to put up enough money to keep Sykes out of court.

13. Residence of Lord Suffield
46 Upper Grosvenor

Another close friend of the prince's, but definitely not deferential, this distinctive gentleman lived around the corner from Lillie Langtry, whom he befriended. Because he shared confidences with the prince, he frequently aided their assignations by providing an excuse for the prince to be making calls in the neighborhood. "It is difficult," he agreed, "to escape the vigilance of our neighbor's eyes."

Return to Park Street and turn left, then turn left again onto Reeves Mews.

14. Site of Lillie Langtry's Residence
Norfolk Square (now Reeves Mews)

This little street that once ran between Park Street and Grosvenor Square was eliminated to make way for modern buildings, but it is likely that Reeves mews were once the mews for Norfolk Street. During her reign as London society's most adored butterfly, Lillie Langtry lived here in a ten-room, red-brick house with stable and mews that was in keeping with similar houses still standing along Park Street.

Even though the Jersey Lily, as she was called, lived the most public of lives, she remains to this day an enigma. At the beginning of her stage career, her devoted friend, Prime Minister Gladstone, said, "My dear, you will receive attacks, personal and critical, just and unjust. Bear them. Never reply and, above all, never rush into print to explain or defend yourself." She never did. And perhaps that is why history has been unable to determine whether this fabulous beauty, this royal mistress, actress, racehorse owner, squanderer of fortunes and collector of lovers was a calculating, coldhearted creature capitalizing on her beauty; or an independent, prideful woman determined to meet adversity on her own terms and win.

Lillie came to London in 1877 from the British island of Jersey off the coast of France as the young, disenchanted second wife of an alcoholic widower who was supported, reluctantly, by his father, a shipbuilder in Belfast. The Langtrys first rented a modest flat on Eaton Place. They had no London friends until, at the opening of the exhibition park housing the Royal Aquarium and the Summer and Winter Garden, Lillie was recognized by Lord Ranelagh, an acquaintance of her father, the Dean of Jersey. Lord Ranelagh invited her to a garden party, at which she met Lady Sebright, a party giver who liked to mingle artists, bohemian intellectuals and new faces with her aristocrats. Lady Sebright was struck with Lillie's fresh beauty, and the next day an invitation arrived to attend one of her Sunday evenings at 23 Lowndes Square in Belgravia. It changed Lillie's life forever.

This was the night Whistler, John Millais, Frank Miles, and Frederick Leighton, London's most prominent artists, discovered the new beauty in their midst, and all vied for the honor of portraying her for posterity. And it was through the artist Miles that she subsequently met Oscar Wilde, whose poetry recorded his devotion to her for posterity.

Lillie had recently lost her favorite brother and was in mourning. Her simple black gown, enormously flattering, set her apart from the flamboyant costumes worn by other beauties, as did her natural poise and lack of affectation. It was not long before she came to the attention of the Prince of Wales, always on the lookout for a new beauty to conquer. Only this time the beauty conquered him. And where the Prince of Wales led, society followed.

Lillie Langtry.

Lillie was the first of the prince's publicly acknowledged mistresses. In those times a royal considered it his seignorial right to court any lady who interested him, although discretion was observed. Husbands, who benefited from royal patronage in indirect ways, took no offense. Lillie's husband simply sank deeper than ever into his bottle.

Perhaps by means of those "indirect ways" in which cuckolded husbands benefited, Edward Langtry suddenly acquired the means to announce that their elevated social status called for more impressive living quarters. To Lillie's delight, they moved from their flat on Eaton Place to a house in this elite Park Lane neighborhood. Her friend Jimmy Whistler helped her decorate it with gilt palm-leaf fans to cover the drab walls, and a ceiling on which he painted drifting white clouds and bright yellow birds in full flight.

The prince's dalliance with Lillie lasted a lusty four years until new temptations arose, but his friendship continued for a lifetime. As their romance waned, on her part as well as his, she met his handsome young nephew, Prince Louis of Battenberg (later Mountbatten), an officer in the British navy presently on leave.

It was love at first sight. Only one obstacle prevented fulfillment. Lillie, although by this time separated, was still married to Edward Langtry. Furthermore the Battenberg family would never have accepted marriage to a divorced woman, nor would the navy. Still, Prince Louis was willing to forfeit his career. He begged the Prince of Wales to intervene and persuade Edward Langtry to agree to a divorce. Instead the Prince of Wales had his nephew assigned to a man-of-war destined for a two-year duty at sea.

It was then Lillie discovered she was pregnant. She confided her secret only to friends Oscar Wilde and Lady Cornwallis-West. When the Prince of Wales inadvertently learned of her condition from her doctor, who also treated the royal family, he hastened to offer financial aid. Lillie accepted temporarily, but was determined to find a way to support herself. The Prince of Wales agreed that his cousin, the father, should never learn of the child she bore. (Most, had they known, would have suspected it was his own.)

Meanwhile Edward Langtry had disappeared, leaving enormous debts. Lillie lived in constant dread that he would learn of her pregnancy and attempt to claim the child. To resolve the dilemma, Patsy Cornwallis-West accompanied Lillie to Ruthyn Castle in Wales, Patsy's family holding, to give birth in secret, while Wilde oversaw the auctioning of her furnishings in the London house and announced to the gossipy press that Mrs. Langtry had decided to retire from social life and move to the country.

That might have spelled "the end" for most nineteenth-century ladies, but not for Lillie. After the birth of Jeanne Marie, she took the child and a competent nanny to her mother in Jersey and returned to London to begin a new life, which we shall learn about in our Belgravia walk.

Continue east on Reeves Mews and Adam's Row to Carlos Place.

15. Residence of Oscar Wilde
9 Carlos Place

In 1881 Frank Miles's father, a canon in the church, caused a rift between Wilde and his son, and Wilde was forced to move from the house they then shared in Chelsea. He chose rooms on the third floor of this corner house, remodeled in 1927 and now used for offices. The walls were oak paneled and decorated with old engravings in depressing black frames. Wilde was unhappy without his famous blue vases and other bric-a-brac. Moreover he was discovering the fallacy of his oft-quoted epigram: "Give me the luxuries; the necessities will take care of themselves." Poetry was not lucrative. The necessities were not taking care of themselves.

Then came a bonanza. *Patience* was playing to record houses in New York. It occurred to entrepreneur D'Oyly Carte that to protect his interest in Gilbert and Sullivan operas, a lucrative sideline might be to introduce to America the famous "aesthete" parodied in the opera. The notion was translated into action, and in November of 1881, Wilde received a welcome contract for a series of lectures in the United States with the understanding that he was to be paraded as a figure in English society, not just as a poet. He had himself costumed by a furrier with a "befrogged and wonderfully befurred green overcoat and Polish cap" and set to work preparing a course of lectures on the modern artistic movements in England.

After returning to London, he continued to live on Carlos Place briefly with his bride while they awaited completion of a new house in Chelsea, purchased with money she brought to the marriage.

Follow Carlos Place south to Mount Street, one of our favorite thoroughfares in Mayfair. En route is the elegant Connaught, the epitome of a late nineteenth-century luxury hotel. Turn west on Mount Street. Street-level shop windows in the gabled Victorian terra-cotta brick houses along here display museum-quality antiques and accoutrements designed to appeal to Mayfair residents. On the south side of the street watch carefully for a small passageway that leads into Mount Street Mansions, a grand development of old Victorian buildings set around a large, quiet park. The benches along its paths are inscribed with the names of donors from all over the world who have enjoyed respite from city noise in this enchanting, unexpected spot. After a rest continue window shopping west along Mount Street to Park Street, and then turn south to South Street.

16. Residence of Catherine Walters (Skittles) 15 South Street

This relatively modest, but attractive, four-story house was the residence of the last of the Victorian courtesans, popularly known as "Skittles." Born in the slums of Liverpool, she emerged into society when her beauty attracted a businessman who established her in London. It was common practice in the 1860s for attractive prostitutes who were also skilled horsewomen to advertise livery stables in Mayfair by riding among the fashionable gentlemen on Rotten Row in Hyde Park. Skittles joined the "pretty horse breakers." Dressed in a skintight riding habit with top hat, she looked both well bred and seductive, in spite of her coarse language.

With one quick look young Hartington (popularly known as Harty-Tarty) fell hopelessly in love. The affair ultimately grew so serious that the young Marquis of Hartington was sent away by his parents to America to inspect the Civil War. On his return his family presented Skittles with the South Street house in Mayfair, carriages, servants and an irrevocable two thousand pounds a year for life to encourage her to discourage Hartington from marrying her. Meanwhile Skittles's Sunday afternoon tea parties attracted some of the most eminent politicians and aristocrats in the country, including Gladstone, Kitchener and the Prince of Wales, who called upon her frequently.

After having broken up with Skittles, Hartington took on another mistress, Louise Manchester, who was married to a duke. Their affair lasted thirty years before the duke died. Louise, then free to marry her longtime lover Hartington (by that time also a duke), became known as the "Double Duchess." To her credit she outlived Harty-Tarty and continued paying the allotment to Skittles until Skittles died in 1920 at age eighty-one.

During her "active" years Skittles's devastating charms were not confined entirely to Harty-Tarty. After the breakup she took a trip to Paris to find solace with another ardent admirer—Wilfrid Scawen Blunt, who was there temporarily on a diplomatic assignment. Although this popular ladies' man fancied himself a poet, his foremost talent lay in the breeding of Arabian horses. As the developer of the Crabbett Arab stud line, he had attracted Lady Anne Milbanke, the horse-loving granddaughter of poet Lord Byron. In deference to her, Skittles again was displaced, but only briefly. After the wedding and birth of one child, Lady Anne's passion for horses became so intense that she reportedly retired at night fully equipped for riding—top boots and all—in order to be ready to mount in the early hours. When ill, she called a vet instead of a doctor. Her other passion was for the violin, which she practiced diligently, never playing anything but scales. When Lady Anne preceded Blunt in death, she neglected to will him her share of the stud line, which initiated scenes with his strongwilled daughter worthy of King Lear.

Blunt built a lovely house for his family near Buckingham Palace, but understandably preferred for himself quarters near Skittles in a Victorian establishment on Mount Street, which he maintained to indulge little "indiscretions." One of these was reported by a shy friend of his daughter's, who as a teenager had fallen madly in love with Blunt, then fifty-three. Even in her own old age, she longingly recalled how she had been captivated by his dark eyes, which seemed to speak his thoughts, and how he would appear for their romantic assignations garbed in an Arab cloak and headdress, like some splendid chieftain.

Actually it wasn't only to capture hearts that Blunt affected Arab dress. He was handsome and vain and would dress up at the twist of a turban, even going so far as to have himself buried rolled up in his favorite oriental carpet. It was suspected that he saw himself as a pure-blooded stallion, servicing fortunate mares in his Mount Street stable, like the fine Arab bloodstock he bred.

After his death in 1922, Blunt's diaries revealed delicious gossip that had come his way via rendezvous with his paramours. One particularly juicy item, which Skittles had relayed to him directly from her friend, the Prince of Wales, concerned Queen Victoria and her favorite, John Brown. This John Brown, a handsome but rather uncouth fellow, had eyes much like Victoria's late prince consort, Albert. The queen, who had been passionately in love with her husband, got the idea that somehow Albert's spirit had passed into Brown.

Brown, ignominiously called "the queen's stallion" by her household, was the reason she spent so much time at Balmoral. They used to retire to a little house in the hills where, on the pretense that he was there "to look after the dogs," he had a bedroom next to hers, while the ladies-in-waiting reclined at the other end of the building. That was the gossip. How true it was, no one will ever know.

What *is* known is that when the Prince of Wales became King Edward VII, one of his first commands was for the destruction of all the statues, busts, cairns and plaques which Queen Victoria had had erected to the memory of her beloved gillie, John Brown, whom her son detested.

During Wilde's trial, with his future threatened by prison, he had occasion to remember Blunt, who had once served a short prison term for his political convictions on Ireland. "Prison had an admirable effect on Blunt as a poet," Wilde observed. "By sending him to gaol, Mr. Balfour converted a clever rhymer into an earnest and deep-thinking poet."

Upon hearing of Wilde's death in Paris, Blunt noted in his diary, "He was without exception the most brilliant talker I have ever come across, the most ready, the most witty, the most audacious. Something of his wit is reflected in his plays, but very little."

Continue east on South Street, crossing South Audley, where on the corner stands a fine old British institution, T. Good Limited Co., specializing in glass objects, vases, pottery and items for home décor. The tall red terra-cotta brick building dates back to 1875 and is a paragon of Victoriana, with cupids, curlicues, niches for vases and countless other gimmicky garnishes along its upper stories. Continue a short distance eastward to the corner of Farm Street and Archibald Mews.

17. The Punch Bowl
Farm Street

This pub is frequented more by locals than tourists. The Punch Bowl is a 250-year-old public house that once was a magistrate's court, where sheep stealers who preyed upon Shepherd Market were brought to trial. In the rear room where lunch is served, a tiny square window opens into the bar section. It was through this opening that sentence was passed from the magistrate's chamber to the prisoner, who, if guilty, was hauled off to the gallows at Tyburn. The walls above the dados in this charming pub are enhanced with wallpaper of typical William Morris design.

Leaving Farm Street, follow Chesterfield Hill south, cross Charles Street and continue down to Curzon Street, where you turn right. Beyond Chesterfield Gardens, a cul-de-sac, turn left off Curzon and work your way down to Hertford Street, and then east into the lively maze of Shepherd Market. En route you will pass:

18. Residence of Rachel and Julius Beer
7 Chesterfield Gardens

Beer inherited *The Observer* and the *Sunday Times* from his father and further embellished his fortune by marrying Rachel Sassoon. Their elegant house, which still stands, boasts one of Mayfair's most imposing Adam staircases. Beer was a hopeless hypochondriac. Rachel had to keep the draperies drawn because light dazzled him, but no oculist could find a defect. Her early training as a nurse very likely had prompted his attraction to her. She soothed him by playing Chopin when the sleeping draughts failed and catered to him unceasingly. When he began to show all the signs of incipient *folie de grandeur,* she closed her eyes to the truth and humored him cheerfully, even when he insisted upon having the Beer family crest clipped out on his black poodle's back.

Eventually Rachel had to take charge. She became editor of both the *Sunday Times* and *The Observer.* The courage she displayed over the controversial Dreyfus Affair and her handling of Esterhazy's confession earned her an honored place in journalistic history. After her husband's death she secluded herself and never really recovered from her grief.

19. Residence of Edward Bulwer-Lytton
36 Hertford Street

A novelist and good friend of the young Disraeli, Bulwer-Lytton lived here with his wife Rosina, who had been a protégé of the writer Caroline Lamb, Bulwer-Lytton's former mistress and also a mistress of the poet Byron. Theirs was a terrible marriage and precipitated a quarrel between Bulwer-Lytton and Disraeli's future wife, Mary Anne, over the mismatched couple's separation.

It was at a Bulwer-Lytton party that Disraeli first met Mary Anne Lewis, then the wife of a rich Welsh coal miner. She told Disraeli that she liked "silent, melancholy men." Noting that she was gifted with unequaled volubility, he answered, "Of that I have no doubt!" never dreaming that he would one day marry her.

Shepherd Market

Shepherd Market, laid out in the eighteenth century, is now a warren of shops and stalls with obvious remnants of a former "red light" reputation. It is a tourist hangout, with a broad array of pubs, snack bars and souvenir shops, usually crowded at lunchtime. Wend your way back to Curzon Street.

20. Residence of Lord Robert Crewe-Milnes
15 Curzon Street

Now the Saudi Arabian Embassy, this eighteenth-century stucco mansion in a tree-studded setting once belonged to the third Lord Crewe, a tyrant praised in Victorian society for his well-ordered household. Crewe firmly stipulated that no housemaids were to be seen in his establishment at any time of the day, except in chapel. Grates were to be tidied, fires laid and lit, downstairs rooms dusted and polished, cans of hot water delivered for bathing, tea made, chamber pots scalded, clothes put away, doorbells answered, beds turned down at night, hot-water bottles filled, curtains drawn and countless incidental duties performed by little genies after nightfall or before dawn, all for the sum of sixteen pounds a year.

21. Residence of Benjamin Disraeli, Earl of Beaconsfield
19 Curzon Street

The colorful prime minister and novelist died in this relatively modest house, having at long last proven beyond a doubt his early tenet that "personal distinction is the only passport to the society of the great."

Continue along Curzon to Queen Street, which leads into Charles Street. (Queen Street is where Harriette Wilson lived, the courtesan whose blackmail threats prompted the Duke of Wellington's famous "publish and be damned" statement.)

22. Residence of Archibald Philip Primrose Rosebery
20 Charles Street

The Prince of Wales and his younger brother, the Duke of Edinburgh, once opened themselves up to a cool rebuke by asking the young Lord Rosebery to lend them his Berkeley Square house for gambling parties and rendezvous with actresses. The Prince of Wales got even, though, after he had become King Edward VII. On an occasion when Lord Rosebery, now prime minister, arrived at an evening reception at Buckingham Palace in trousers instead of the formal knee breeches worn at court functions, the king was furious. "I presume," he said in his guttural voice, "that you have come in the suit of the American ambassador."

Lord Rosebery was the second gentile to break the rigid tradition of Rothschild women marrying only in the Jewish faith when he took as his bride Hannah Rothschild, only child of Mayer. Hannah died twelve years later. Lord Rosebery never remarried, but after he had become prime minister, he aspired to marry Princess Victoria. Both were very lonely and could have been happy, except for tyrannical, possessive Queen Alexandra, who refused to let her daughter go. Not until the princess was a sick old lady was she allowed her own apartment in Kensington Palace.

23. I Am the Only Running Footman
Charles Street

This pub, located on a charming Mayfair street, bears the truly unique sign of a liveried footman, whose duty it was to run before an aristocrat's carriage in the days before automobiles and paved streets. His tasks included paying tolls, carrying lights at night, and alerting drivers to road conditions. Dressed in white and carrying staffs, the footmen were picturesque and athletic. Many could cover twenty miles in times not far from record breaking. Their work was necessary, for the bad condition of the roads and their uncertain width frequently made it impossible for carriages to pass each other except at recognized places. Mayfair residents employed a fair number of these men. It was their custom to meet at the inn in Charles Street.

In a few sections of London, we have a hard time finding a pub we like. In Mayfair we have a hard time finding one we don't like. The Running Footman is one we happily return to.

24. Residence of Consul E. Nevill-Rolfe and Lady Dorothy Nevill
45 Berkeley Square

Continue along Charles Street to Berkeley Square, shaded by plane trees dating back to 1789 when this was a wooded glen. At the turn of the century, it was among the most aristocratic squares in London. The statue in the square's center is by A. Munro, 1867. A number of the old stone-faced mansions have been demolished, but those which remain are still embellished by ironwork across first-floor balconies and lovely lamp holders with torch snuffers at their entrance steps.

Number 45 is where Lady Dorothy Nevill received Gladstone, Disraeli and other celebrities of her day. Her husband, the consul in Naples, saw Wilde when Wilde had taken a villa there for a short time in 1897, after exiling himself from England. The consul wrote to his London neighbor, Lord Rosebery, "Wilde lives a completely secluded life, using the name Mr. Sebastian Nothwell. He looks thoroughly abashed, much like a whipped hound. He has written a volume of poems, but no one in London would publish them and I hear he is printing them at his own expense."

From Berkeley Square follow Bruton Street to New Bond Street and window-shop your way north on one side of the street up to Brook Street, which leads on the east into Hanover Square.

25. St. George's Church
Hanover Square

St. George's is considered the West End's most impressive church. It was built from 1713 to 1724 by John James, a follower of Christopher Wren. The composer George Frederick Handel had his own pew here. Benjamin Disraeli, Queen Victoria's favorite, married Mrs. Wyndham Lewis here in 1839. J.W. Cross, a New York banker, and Mary Ann Evans (novelist George Eliot) were wed in 1880, and Theodore Roosevelt and Edith Carow in 1886. Nathan Rothschild's disinherited daughter Hannah was reluctantly delivered here for her unattended wedding to the gentile Henry Fitzroy in 1839, while her grieving mother departed in her carriage without so much as a blessing.

It is a lovely, light church inside, all white with details highlighted in gold. The two cast-iron game dogs poised at the entrance present a mystery. No one knows their origin nor their significance in relation to the church.

Bond Street

Now retrace your steps to Bond Street and walk south toward Piccadilly, window shopping the opposite side of the street. This famous shopping street is as exclusive today as it was at the turn of the century, when tightly corsetted ladies surreptitiously purchased Madame Rachel's "Chinese Leaves" for the cheeks and lips, and "Magnetic Rock Dew Water of the Sahara" or "Venus's Toilet." Really two streets, Old Bond and New Bond, they connect, but each has its own confusing number system.

At the cross street of Grafton is the elaborate black, white and gold corner façade of Asprey's, one of London's most luxurious shops for gift items of gold, silver, and leather. Founded in 1781, it was moved to this location in 1887. Asprey's possesses the royal warrant. Wilde made much of the two engraved Asprey cigarette cases he carried at all times.

26. Site of the Aeolian Hall
135-37 New Bond Street

Once the Aeolian Hall, in 1877 this building celebrated the opening of a new gallery by Sir Coutts Lindsay designed not only to present the contemporary art scene more fairly and vivaciously than the jealous Royal Academy, but to constitute a work of art in itself. Accordingly a new Palladian façade was imposed upon its front and Whistler was commissioned to do a frieze on the coved ceiling of the west gallery, depicting in silver against a subdued blue ground the moon in its phases and the accompanying stars. The gallery walls, as Wilde approvingly noted, were "hung with scarlet damask above a dado of dull green-gold." Henry James, observing the strong colors, especially the "savage" red, found them a distracting background for paintings, but Wilde rejoiced in the lavish décor. Today it is still an elegant building, handsomely remodeled and used for offices.

27. Residence of Henry Irving
15A Grafton Street

This great thespian of the nineteenth century occupied rooms on the first and second floors of the building around the corner from, but adjacent to, Asprey's. Engravings on the art of fencing hung over a dark winding staircase leading up to rooms kept in a perpetual state of disorder. Irving lived in twilight, rarely opening the draperies that covered the stained and leaded glass of the windows.

Sir Henry Irving, Ellen Terry's leading man—both on and off the stage.

As an actor, he never hesitated to rewrite or cut Shakespeare, tailoring the script to his own talents. He initiated the device of lowering auditorium lights to focus attention onto the stage, and he continued to use gas lighting for subtle effects even after electricity was available.

At the beginning of his career, Irving was driving along Hyde Park with his wife when she, resentful of his absorption with the theatre, asked, "Are you going to go on making a fool of yourself like this all your life?" Irving left her on the spot, moved to Grafton Street and took over management of the Lyceum Theatre. He never spoke to her again, although he supported her.

His enduring romance with Ellen Terry began when she, after a prolonged absence from the theatre, returned to perform in her first role as his leading lady. When the curtain came down, she fled in panic to her home in Earl's Court, a long distance from the theatre, convinced that she had given a poor performance.

Irving suffered a neurotic fear of being outside alone in the dark. Nevertheless he followed the distraught lady, arriving at her home to reassure her until long past midnight. Perhaps he was afraid to return alone in the dark. At any rate they remained a twosome for many years, both onstage and off.

28. Site of Sir George Chetwynd's Residence
23 Cork Street

On the opposite side of Bond Street from Asprey's, walk a few steps along Clifford Street and turn right into Cork Street. This short thoroughfare is devoted today almost entirely to art galleries. Number 23 has been torn down, but was no doubt built in the style of the existing old residences on the even-numbered side of the street.

Chetwynd, a future senior steward of the Jockey Club, gave Lillie Langtry sage advice on how to keep accounts when she was heavily involved in building her stable of racehorses, as well as on how to appraise at the Monday bloodstock sales at Tattersall's. Even though married with three children, he found her irresistible, which almost led to his social undoing.

One sunny afternoon he discovered to his chagrin that Lillie had favored Lord Hugh Lonsdale as her riding companion over himself. Lividly jealous, Chetwynd promptly stationed himself at the rails alongside Rotten Row to await them. When the riders spotted him, they reined in their horses.

"Stay away from my Lillie," Chetwynd yelled at Lord Lonsdale, whereupon the sporting earl jumped down from his horse and in the tanbark of the Row, the battle began. Chetwynd went down first. His top hat rolled in the dust while the horses shied away in fright, but seconds later he was on his feet exchanging punches, until two gentlemen spectators pulled them apart and packed them off to their homes in closed carriages. The newspapers had a field day with that!

After perusing the Cork Street art galleries, return to Bond Street. Continue the short distance to Piccadilly, from where buses may be boarded to most locations in London.

WALK

MARYLEBONE

FOUR

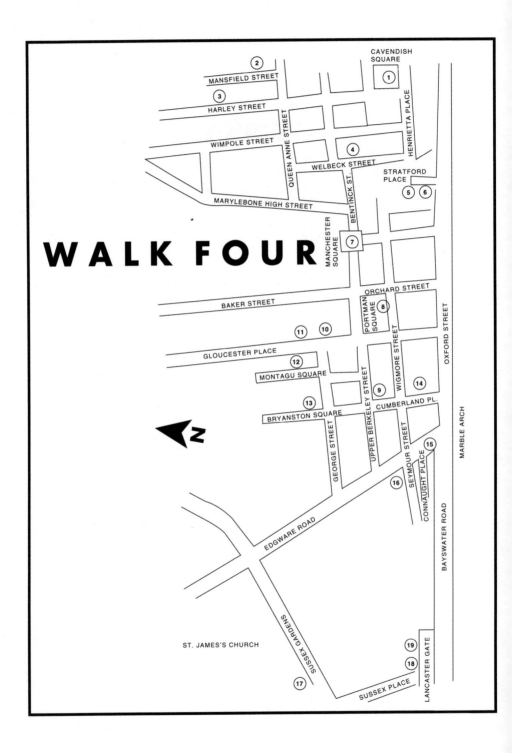

Oxford and Regent Streets

As this walk is primarily through residential districts, it is one we recommend for a quiet Sunday. For the purpose of our walk, Marylebone weaves a long rambling trail north of Oxford Street and Hyde Park from Cavendish Square westward to Sussex Gardens. Begin at the bus stop at Oxford and Regent streets and walk north to Cavendish Square.

Regent Street, near Oxford Circus, in the 1880s.

1. Residence of Herbert Henry Asquith, Earl of Oxford
20 Cavendish Square

In this impressive five-story stone house (now the Royal College of Nursing) which overlooks the square's lovely garden, the Asquiths hosted gatherings of the "Souls" from 1895 to 1908. Prime Minister Asquith was out of office most of the time he lived here and was not returned to government until 1906.

His wife Margot was a prime mover in the Souls, a circle begun in 1888 who reveled in one another's company and considered themselves an intellectual elite, immune to worldly pretensions and interested in discussing only "the worthwhile." Their name was coined by Charles Beresford during a dinner. Turning to Arthur Balfour, Herbert Asquith, Harry Cust, Mary Elcho, Violet, Duchess of Ruthland, and Margot Asquith, he said, "You all sit talking about each other's souls. I shall call you the Souls." Lord Curzon and the womanizing Wilfrid Scawen Blunt (whom we met in Mayfair) later drifted into the circle. The trouble was that during the ten years they met, the Souls too often discovered they had bodies, too, especially with the debonair lady-killer, Harry Cust, present.

Although Wilde held himself aloof from the Souls to a degree, he was friendly with most of the members and occasionally honored them with his presence. His acquaintance with Margot Tennant Asquith had begun in their youth. One of his fairy tales, "The Star-Child," was dedicated to her.

Margot also fancied herself a writer. She wrote her autobiography, but veracity wasn't her strong point. After the death of George V, the king's doctor fell victim to her sharp tongue. "Lord Dawson was not a good doctor," she said. "King George himself told me that he would never have died had he had another doctor."

When Herbert Asquith was prime minister and living at number 10 Downing Street in Westminster, the irrepressible Margot smoked in public and said whatever came into her head, oblivious to the effect she was having on the stodgy middle class. Moreover she invited the modern dancer Maud Allen to perform at a soirée in the sanctity of the prime minister's residence, as a barefoot nymph in Mendelssohn's *Spring Song*. (Bare legs in those days were considered overexciting.) And worse was to come. In the following year Maud danced with a jewel glued in her navel, visible through transparent veils.

In spite of it all, Margot maintained her social prominence, even though she shocked her contemporaries when she mentioned things in public too intimate to print, like her anguish at losing a stillborn baby. One of her peers was heard to say, "I wish Margot did not feel she must even publish her birth pangs." Another friend immediately retorted, "My dear, Margot would publish her hiccoughs!"

Enter Harley Street from Cavendish Square and walk north to Queen Anne Street, turn right for a short distance, and then turn left on Mansfield Street.

2. Residence of Sir Edwin Lutyens
13 Mansfield Street

This charming little street with its gas lamps and iron fences was a choice for several nineteenth-century architects, whose houses are marked by London Historical Society plaques. Of them Lutyens's name is the best known today. With the help of a loan from Lady Sackville, who also gave him a Rolls Royce with chauffeur, Lutyens established a reputation for himself as a residential architect for the affluent middle class. He was employed as a consultant architect to the Westminster estate, and it was he who spread neo-Georgian façades throughout Mayfair. He was also responsible for the Cenotaph in London, as well as some notable town houses.

In 1898 he wed the very-shy Emily Lytton, daughter of Lord Lytton, viceroy to India, whom he met on a country bicycle path (which was a very good thing, since she was about to be seduced by the Arabian-turbaned Blunt in his Mayfair lair). As it turned out, the marriage was disappointing. His desperate efforts to maintain his wife and family in the gracious style they desired occupied too much time, and his shy wife grew lonely.

In search of solace she turned to Theosophy, a popular cult of the time, and grew so involved that she overcame shyness and became a lecturer for its society. A prime motivation for this was another turban-wearing romantic, albeit more spiritual than Blunt. This one, the young Indian Krishnamurti, proclaimed by Theosophists as the precursor of the coming world teacher, appealed to her devotional nature to such an extent that, when he disclaimed his role in 1929, she suffered for the rest of her life.

In contrast her husband amused himself with practical jokes. Once, while visiting the eccentric antiquarian, Sir Osbert Sitwell, he drew some strands of horsehair stuffing from a broken sofa, wrapped them in a piece of paper on which he had written a few words, and quietly deposited them in a desk drawer. Many years later Osbert Sitwell discovered the little package. Upon it was written, "A lock cut from Marie Antoinette's hair ten minutes after the execution."

Return to Harley Street, a prosperous thoroughfare favored by the medical profession, which still maintains its nineteenth-century charm.

3. Residence of Sir Arthur Pinero
115A Harley Street

Pinero's greatest success as a playwright was during the 1880s and 1890s. His first full-length play, *The Money Spinner,* was performed at the St. James's Theatre in 1881 and exposed gambling in polite society. He continued to shock his audiences in *The Second Mrs. Tanqueray,* which was a forthright treatment of the double standards prevalent in the morality of the day. Wilde had a poor opinion of his contemporary dramatists. Commenting on a play by Pinero, he said, "It is the best play I ever slept through."

Judging from the appearance of this fine corner house where Pinero lived from 1909 until his death, he must have managed to keep most of his audiences awake. The white portico marking its entrance is around the corner from Harley Street, on Devonshire.

Continue one block west on Devonshire and turn south on Wimpole Street, where the romantic poet Elizabeth Barrett Browning lived with her strict father at number 50. Continue on to Queen Anne Street and turn right (west) for one block, then continue south on Welbeck Street, a street so typically Victorian that you can almost hear the echo of carriage wheels.

4. Residence of Thomas Woolner
29 Welbeck Street

Sculptor and poet Woolner so admired Dante Gabriel Rossetti that he became a member of Rossetti's Pre-Raphaelite movement. Finding it difficult to live on dreams, he enacted an even greater one by sailing to Melbourne, Australia, in 1852 to seek his fortune in the goldfields. Two years later he returned without a fortune, but his sculpture began to excite attention. Elected to the Royal Academy, he executed many outdoor memorials and produced busts of practically all the eminent men of his time.

To enter Stratford Place, a cul-de-sac, it is necessary to continue south to Oxford Street and turn into it between Marylebone and Gee streets.

5. Stratford House—Residence of Mrs. Henrietta Guthrie
Stratford Place

Now the Oriental Club, it was in this graceful mansion that Mrs. Murray Guthrie first employed the resourceful Rosa

Lewis to cater a ten-course dinner for twenty people. As a result of that success, Rosa was introduced to Lady Randolph Churchill (who told her how to please the palate of the Prince of Wales) and other members of London society. Her clientele indirectly funded the exclusive Cavendish Hotel that the Duchess of Duke Street ultimately opened in St. James's.

6. Residence of Sir Allen Young
5 Stratford Place

It was at a dinner party in this bachelor establishment that the swashbuckling adventurer Sir Allen Young introduced Lillie Langtry to the Prince of Wales on May 24, 1877, a date she would remember for the rest of her life.

Called "Alleno" by his friends, Young had twice at his own expense, in 1875 and a year later, sailed his yacht *Pandora* in a brave, but futile, attempt to discover the Northwest Passage, that elusive arctic sea route joining the Atlantic and Pacific oceans. In recognition of his services, he was knighted in 1877. Shortly after the prince's return from his annual outing to the south of France and Paris, Alleno decided it was time to introduce him to the newest Professional Beauty, who was the talk of the town. Lillie Langtry had no idea, as she donned her little black mourning frock that was beginning to make her so famous, that she would be seated that night next to the prince.

As addicted as Bertie was to beautiful women, it took no time at all for the two of them to establish rapport. Lillie felt rather shaky when she made her curtsy, but he quickly put her at ease by telling her that he had heard she was as fascinating to know as to look at. A breathless moment later he added that in his experience, fascination was related to mystery, and to succumb to it one must have more than a brief encounter. He then politely turned to converse with the person on his other side while Lillie quietly contemplated a "more leisurely encounter."

Take the next right turn off of Oxford and work your way in a northeasterly direction to Manchester Square.

7. The Wallace Collection
Manchester Square

Formerly the home of the Marquess of Hertford, this nineteenth-century town house is now the home of the

Wallace Collection, and one of the most delightful galleries in London. All of the marquesses of Hertford were avid collectors, especially the fourth marquess (1818-90). Many of the treasures were housed in his Paris home until about 1870, when his natural son, Richard Wallace, transferred the entire collection to London. The collection contains beautiful china, French objets d'art, furniture, and eighteenth-century French paintings, in addition to a European armory collection acquired by Richard Wallace. Frans Hals's *The Laughing Cavalier* is a major contribution, as are several Watteau pastorals.

Only a few English artists are represented in the collection, but the house is a treasure in itself, and presents an opportunity to experience the inside of an elegant mansion furnished in the exquisitely refined taste of a Louise Sassoon or a Ferdie Rothschild of the 1890s.

Continue west on Upper Berkeley Street from Manchester Square to Portman Square.

8. Site of Mrs. Alice Keppel's Residence
Portman Square (now the Churchill Hotel)

When the Prince of Wales had reached the age when a man values a good partner at the bridge table as highly as a good partner in bed, Mrs. Alice Keppel had become his acknowledged mistress. She lived with her husband and daughter in a six-story house that boasted few amenities, such as central heating and a telephone, which were found by that time in most comparable houses. She did have electricity instead of gas, however, and the unheard-of luxury of two bathrooms.

In spite of its practical drawbacks, the house was comfortable, and Alice avoided the frivolous fussiness that characterized the fin de siècle décor so popular at the time. Curtains were not drawn until daylight faded, and luxuriously thick rugs, mounds of pillows, Chinese porcelain pagodas and bowers of flowers in cut-glass vases provided an adequately seductive setting for her extramarital assignations, when the prince arrived in an unmarked brougham. Mr. Keppel spent a great deal of time at his club.

After the prince became King Edward VII, Alice Keppel's position remained unaltered. She became one of the leading personalities of his court and a favored bridge partner. On one occasion when he barked at her for having played the wrong card, she boldly countered that she "never could tell a king from a knave."

Their relationship was hardly surreptitious. It was highly visible even to the public. Once, when urgently summoned by the king to meet him at a country house, Mrs. Keppel stepped into a hansom cab with her luggage and directed the cabby to the station: "King's Cross," she said.

"Is he—oh dear!" said the cabby, whipping up his horse. "Where do you want to go?"

The king asked for her on his deathbed and she attended his last farewell, much to the vexation of Queen Alexandra.

Continue west on Upper Berkeley Street from Portman Square.

9. Site of Mary Leslie Crawshay's Residence
Upper Berkeley Street (now also part of the Churchill Hotel)

A sequel to the fragmented romance of Lord Rosebery and Princess Victoria was revealed by a descendant of Mary Leslie Crawshay. The astringent old lady, who always said "self-pity is like sitting in wet shoes," still lamented the fate of her friend, the princess. "If you knew what royalties have to endure and never show it!" she once exclaimed to her niece. In the early 1830s the husbandless princess had come to her house for tea. The princess had confessed that there had been someone so perfect for her, but she had not been allowed to marry him. Then her voice had broken and she had added, "And we *could* have been so happy."

Turn back toward Portman Square and walk north up Gloucester Place. On the corner of Gloucester Place and George Street, you may want to stop for a lager at the Worcester Pub, especially on a nice summer day when tables are outside. The next three streets we want to visit all run north from George Street—Gloucester, Montagu Square and Bryanston Square.

10. Residence of William Wilkie Collins
65 Gloucester Place

Off and on from 1868 to 1888, Collins lived here with one or another of his mistresses. He achieved popularity with his mystery story, *The Woman in White,* which was adapted for the stage, but had little appeal for English audiences. Collins suffered with gout and took increasing amounts of opium to dull the pain. By the time he started *The Mooonstone,* he was taking enough opium to "put a dinner party of twelve under the table." He was a radical and ardent womanizer and braved Victorian morals by living with one mistress and keeping another in a separate establishment.

11. Residence of Elizabeth Barrett Browning
91 Gloucester Place

A block along the street from Collins, but many years earlier, Mrs. Browning lived at this address after her marriage. Today she is more famed for her romance with Robert Browning than for her own poetry, although when they married and fled to Italy, she was the more famous.

Her invalid life was the result of a riding accident which damaged her spine. It was exacerbated by the strict regime imposed by her father in their family home at 50 Wimpole Street; he refused to consider marriage for any of his daughters. Before her elopement she summed up her predicament and her frustration as a writer because of it: "A bird in a cage would have as good a story; most of my events and nearly all of my intense pleasure have passed in my thoughts."

Excitement came into her life with her secret marriage to her fiery poet lover in 1846. The Brownings lived in Florence in 1850 and Elizabeth published *Sonnets from the Portuguese,* forty-four love poems to Robert. While at Oxford, Wilde had praised Elizabeth Barrett Browning's *Aurora Leigh* "as much as the greatest work in literature," but later in his career, he found that her work no longer interested him.

12. Residence of Anthony Trollope
39 Montagu Square

In 1873 Trollope moved into this attractive large house, with its wrought-iron gate, first-floor balcony and bay window overlooking the square's fenced, private garden. It was "the house for which I hope to live and hope to die," he wrote. His first act in the new home was to organize his library of five thousand books, because he said "they are dearer to me even than the horses which are going, or than the wine in the cellar, which is very apt to go, and upon which I also pride myself." When the books were shelved, he began a novel, *The Way We Live Now,* a satire which explored the inroads of the speculative financier into English and political life. He made a very adequate income from his writing, but left Wilde unimpressed. "He leaves no echoes," Wilde observed.

He did leave one important legacy, however—one that echoes to this day. To augment his income in the early days, he served as a clerk in the juvenescent General Post Office and is credited with the invention of the letter box. Now this may seem an ordinary contribution today, but before telephones were common, the standing, iron letter box was the prime aid to communication, with postal pickups numbering fifteen a day. A letter dropped in the morning or early afternoon would reach any London address on that day. The boxes then, as now, are as distinctive to London as the red double-decker buses, and are the same color. The earliest ones were embossed with the insignia "VR," for Victoria Regina, in raised script. Although rare, some still stand on London streets. Later ones have insignias of George VI or Elizabeth II.

13. Residence of Ian Malcolm and Jeanne Marie Langtry
5 Bryanston Square

The spacious terrace house on this gracious gas-lamp-lit square became the home of Lillie Langtry's estranged daughter following her marriage in 1902 to Ian Malcolm. Jeanne Marie had grown up largely on the island of Jersey, where she lived with her grandmother. It wasn't until she accompanied Lillie on one of her American tours that Jeanne Marie learned Lillie, whom she had always called "auntie," was really her mother. And it wasn't until the eve of Jeanne Marie's wedding that Lillie confessed the identity of Jeanne Marie's real father, Prince Louis Battenberg. Until then she had assumed she was the daughter of a mysterious Edward Langtry, whom she'd never met.

Jeanne Marie was properly introduced into society and presented at court, sponsored by Lillie's loyal friends, Lady Patsy Cornwallis-West and Lady de Grey, with the Prince of Wales looking out for her interests. On June 30, 1902 she married the Honorable Ian Malcolm, heir to impeccable social credentials and a vast estate in Scotland.

Although Louis Battenberg was preferable as a father to a drunken sot like Langtry, her illegitimacy caused Jeanne Marie great pain. She never forgave her mother. Lillie gave her away at the wedding, but afterward Jeanne Marie informed her that she wished never to meet her again. She never did.

Ian Malcolm went on to a successful parliamentary career and in time was knighted, making Jeanne Marie "Lady Malcolm."

Follow Great Cumberland Place southward to Marble Arch.

14. Residence of Leonie Leslie
46 Great Cumberland Place

This terrace house was the home of a true romantic, a dear friend and inamorata of the Duke of Connaught, the brother of the Prince of Wales. She formerly had lived at number 10. During its destruction she sadly threw a rose into its ruins. When she told George Du Maurier, he was so touched that it inspired him to include the sentimental incident in a story.

At the Marble Arch, cross Edgware Road to Connaught Place.

15. Residence of Lord Randolph and Jennie Jerome Churchill
2 Connaught Place

A fracas with the Prince of Wales over a scandal brought about Churchill's temporary ostracism from society and precipitated his acceptance of an appointment as the queen's viceroy to trouble-torn Ireland. When he and his American-born wife Jennie, whom he had married in 1874, finally returned to London with their young son Winston, they moved into this lovely white Georgian mansion overlooking Hyde Park. It was Jennie who, after ten years of enmity, effected a reconciliation between the two former friends when the prince accepted her invitation to a supper party in 1886.

Churchill already had established his reputation as a brilliant parliamentary orator, and after the defeat of the Conservatives in 1880 came forward as the leader of the Fourth party, a group pledged to uphold true Tory principles. In 1886 he became leader of the House of Commons.

An amusing story is told about a time in Westminster when Lord Randolph was buttonholed on the stairs by a bore who embarked upon a long-winded tale. Finally Lord Randolph summoned a footman. "Listen until his lordship finishes," he instructed the man, and then made his own escape.

The Churchill marriage was destined for tragedy when Lord Randolph contracted syphilis. Jennie did not know about it and couldn't understand why he had left her bed. She fell in love with a delightful Austrian, Count Charles Kinsky, to make up for Randolph's neglect. After her husband's death she married the much-younger son of one of her contemporaries, Lady Patsy Cornwallis-West. He eventually became enamored of the glamorous Mrs. Patrick Campbell and abandoned Jennie to marry the actress.

16. Tyburn Pub
Edgware Road

A short block from Connaught Place, on the corner of Edgware Road and Seymour Street, is this pleasant pub with street-side tables, from which you may watch the most cosmopolitan parade in London. This district near the Marble Arch represents a melting pot of races that exceeds anything in America. Tiny markets and restaurants along Edgware Road cater to the exotic tastes of Moroccans dressed in djellabas, purdah-clad Pakistanis draped with black face veils, Mozambique women crowned with striped scarves, sheikhs in pink turbans, Hindus in saris, and Middle Eastern Muslims fingering worry beads. It is hard, here, to believe that you are in London.

The remaining addresses included in the Marylebone walk are more interesting to read about than to see, as the walk is long and the former Harte and Lloyd residences are now lodging houses or small economy hotels. If your feet are about to give out and you choose not to continue, there are bus stops on Edgware Road or the Marble Arch underground station a short walk away. Should you wish to continue, walk north on Edgware Road to Sussex Gardens, turn left, and continue on to St. James's Church.

17. St. James's Church
Sussex Gardens

Oscar Wilde married his violet-eyed Constance Lloyd in this charming little church on May 29, 1884. It was an intimate wedding with only family and close friends attending. Jimmy Whistler, Oscar's closest friend at the time, sent a telegram to the church. "Fear I may not be able to reach you in time for the ceremony. Don't wait."

Oscar himself, costumed to resemble George IV in breeches and buckled shoes, designed the bridal gown—rich creamy satin with a delicate cowslip tint, low square-cut bodice, high Medici collar, and large puffed sleeves— all set off by a silver girdle of beautiful workmanship, the gift of the groom. A saffron-colored Indian gauze veil embroidered with pearls, and a thick wreath of myrtle leaves and white blossoms completed the ensemble. Equally overdressed were the bridesmaids. Oscar was pleased when *The World* reported it as "a wedding in the high aesthetic mode."

The happy couple then left for a honeymoon in Paris.

From the church, turn left onto Lancaster Terrace and follow it to Lancaster Gate.

18. Residence of Bret Harte
74 Lancaster Gate

The American story writer whose forte was the Old West lived in this house, now an unpretentious lodging house, from

Bret Harte, the American writer as he was portrayed in Vanity Fair *on January 4, 1879, before he came to England.*

1895 to 1902. The house was designed by Sancton Wood and built in 1887.

Harte chose to remain in London when he was relieved of consulate duty in Scotland, where he had spent about four years. When he first came to Europe, his wife and family remained in New York. Before he died in an English friend's country house, however, his wife and daughter had moved to London, but it was believed that their separation was permanent and they made it a point never to meet, although he supported them. The reason for their parting was a carefully guarded secret and has never been revealed.

Oscar Wilde, caricatured by Pellegrini in 1884, (courtesy of the National Portrait Gallery).

It is doubtful that Harte was acquainted with Wilde, but Wilde was delighted with one of his stories: "The aim of most of our modern novelists seems to be, not to write good novels, but to write novels that will do good," Wilde complained. "It was therefore pleasant," he continued, "to come across a heroine in Bret Harte's 'Cressy' who is not identified with any great cause, and represents no important principle." After that accolade, though, Wilde followed with a characteristic barb, adding, "We sincerely hope that a few more novels like this will be published, as the public will then find out that a bad book is very dear at a shilling."

19. Residence of John Horatio Lloyd
100 Lancaster Gate

Constance Lloyd had been unhappy at home after her widowed mother's remarriage, so she lived in Dublin with her grandfather, John Horatio Lloyd, from whom she stood to inherit a modest fortune. As a member of the Queen's Council, Lloyd also maintained a London mansion at 100 Lancaster Gate, watched over by a maiden niece. Both of these relatives opposed her desire to marry Wilde, who had meager financial prospects, until Oscar managed to charm the grandfather. The aunt never did favor him, but allowed Constance to stay at the Lancaster Gate house until the wedding.

Wilde courted Constance ardently, and there is little doubt that he was in love with her. Lesser known than many of his poems, but perhaps more sincere, is this one he sent to Constance:

> *I can write no stately proem*
> *As a prelude to my lay;*
> *From a poet to a poem*
> *I would dare to say.*
>
> *For if of these fallen petals*
> *One to you seem fair,*
> *Love will waft it till it settles*
> *On your hair.*
>
> *And when wind and winter harden*
> *All the loveless land,*
> *It will whisper of the garden,*
> *"You will understand."*

Bayswater Road at Lancaster Gate is a major bus route for your return to central London.

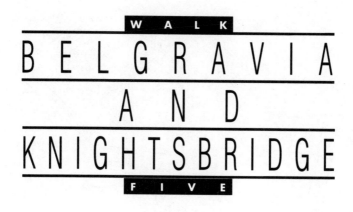

WALK

BELGRAVIA AND KNIGHTSBRIDGE

FIVE

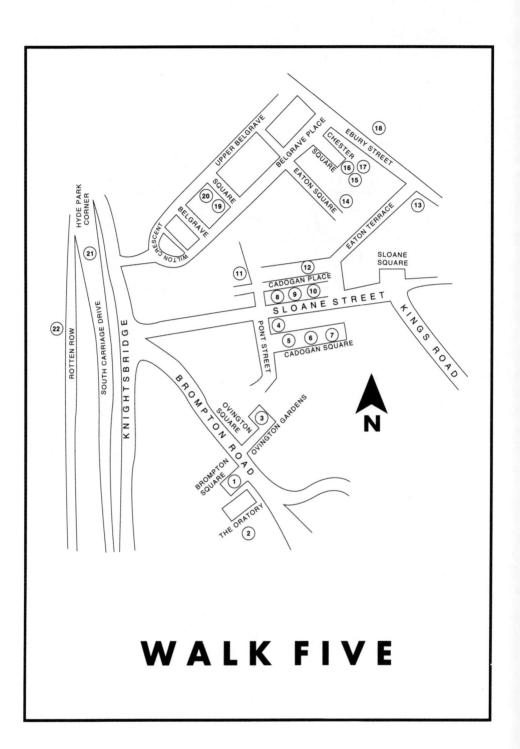

WALK FIVE

Harrods Department Store

This walk begins at Harrods Department Store on Brompton Road, reached by any Knightsbridge-bound bus.

Belgravia and Knightsbridge are synonymous today with elegant living and shopping, but prior to the nineteenth century, this was an unkempt village outside London, a place for cattle markets and slaughterhouses. Then a small grocer named Harrod took steps to assure the area's future by anticipating a farsighted developer, who was establishing Georgian-style residential squares there. By 1905 Harrod had prospered enough that he could dominate his block by building the terra-cotta brick store crowned with towers and cupolas that is a landmark (and focus) for London shoppers today. Its food halls, once so dear to Harrod's heart, are showplaces of art nouveau tile decoration as well as sumptuous food and not to be missed.

After tearing yourself away from Harrods, continue west along Brompton Road and cross to Brompton Square.

1. Residence of Stéphane Mallarmé
6 Brompton Square

Mallarmé, the French poet best known for his "L'Après-Midi d'un Faune," came to London in 1862 to learn English. He met a German governess, Marie Gerhard, whom he married, and they remained in London for two years. Mallarmé was influenced by the English romantic poets, particularly Keats, Shelley and Coleridge, but following their footsteps in England didn't spawn inspiration, as he had hoped. Instead he found it a constant struggle to compose poetry in the conditions of poverty he saw around him. After leaving London, he taught English in Paris for the rest of his life. Wilde met him in Paris and attended two of the poet's famous *mardis.*

By 1890 the decadents among French writers were moving toward symbolism, and Mallarmé was a leader. His influence on Wilde is evident in the preface of *Dorian Gray,* which Wilde was writing at the time of his Paris visit: "All art is at once surface and symbol. Those who go beneath the surface do so at their peril. Those who read the symbol do so at their peril."

Both Mallarmé and Wilde saw literature as the supreme art, one that could transform a painting into words. And both were somewhat obsessed with the theme of Salome. Mallarmé's central work, *Herodiade,* based on the theme of Salome, was still unfinished when Wilde embarked upon his *Salomé,* written in French. Whether or not Wilde intended it to compete with Mallarmé's epic poem, it did. In a futile effort to complete *Herodiade,* Mallarmé was forced to recognize Wilde's effort, saying that he would retain the name of *Herodiade* for his work in order to differentiate it from the other *Salomé,* which he described as "modern."

While Wilde grieved in prison, Salomé was finally produced in Paris in 1896 and well received by audience and critics. "It is something that at a time of disgrace and shame I should still be regarded as an artist: I wish I could feel more pleasure; but I seem dead to all emotions except those of anguish and despair," he wrote to his friend Robert Ross.

2. Brompton Oratory
Brompton Road

The huge dome you see further along Brompton Road south of Brompton Square rises above the Brompton Oratory, an Italianate Roman Catholic church built during the mid-Victorian period, when English Catholics and vacillating converts were emerging into the light of tolerance.

Wilde wavered most of his life between the Catholic church, the Protestant church of his parents, or no church at all. The latter won, except on his deathbed, when he finally opted for Catholicism. Earlier, however, during a fit of sickness at Oxford in 1878, he had experienced an attack of anxiety about his soul. A month after having been confined to his bed, he went to speak confidentially to the fashionable priest, Reverend Sebastian Bowden, at the Brompton Oratory in London. Bowden was well known for his conversions among London's social set.

After Wilde's confession the priest wrote a letter urging him to "obey God's call promptly and cheerfully," promising that his difficulties would disappear after his conversion, and that true happiness would begin. An appointment for another meeting was set for the following Thursday. At last Wilde was forced to the point of decision. On Thursday, when Wilde was to be received into the church, in lieu of Wilde, a large package arrived addressed to the priest. In it was a spray of lilies, Wilde's polite way of "flowering over" his renunciation.

In *The Picture of Dorian Gray,* Wilde's character, Lord Henry Wotton, is more cynical, but Wilde may have drawn from his own experience. "Religion consoles some," Lord Henry says. "Its mysteries have all the charm of a flirtation . . . . Besides, nothing makes one so vain as being told that one is a sinner."

From Brompton Square cross to Ovington Square on the opposite side of Brompton Road.

3. Residence of Lady "Speranza" Wilde
1 Ovington Square

When her tenants in Dublin failed to pay their rent on her properties, Lady Wilde and Willie, Oscar's older brother, came to join Oscar in London. After settling at Ovington Square, she inaugurated her Saturday afternoon salons, at which she presided over a tea table that dispensed more Irish whiskey than tea.

Although Oscar was the chief drawing card, Willie, who worked off and on as a journalist, gave him enough competition to build a little tension. Once, when asked what he was working at, Willie responded "at intervals." He was an inch taller than Oscar's six feet, two inches and closely resembled him. Oscar, however, was very resentful when acquaintances confused them.

Most of Lady Wilde's guests were Irish newcomers, like George Bernard Shaw and W.B. Yeats, who gathered here to meet people and were grateful for Lady Wilde's hospitality. Others came to laugh at the eccentric lady but stayed to marvel. Lady Wilde, wearing a black wig topped with exotic headdresses, and garbed in costumes of the 1860s, with large flounces, beads and pendants, was a delightful, if quixotic, hostess, always ready with a quip that would bear repeating and spread her name around town. In an oracular mood she once announced, "I have come to the conclusion that nothing in the world is worth living for except . . ." she paused before hissing out the last word . . ."sin!"

When Wilde's fame was at its zenith in the nineties and he could no longer find time to attend his mother's functions, the celebrities disappeared, and Lady Wilde seemed to exhibit greater dignity. She no longer painted her face, and her manner became somewhat aloof, but she spoke with pride of her successful son. "The world will not leave him alone," she said, explaining his rare visits. She and Willie then moved to Oakley Street in Chelsea.

At the south end of the square, cross over to Pont Street.

4. Residence of Sir George Alexander
57 Pont Street

This impressive building, now the Executive Hotel, was once the home of Sir George Alexander, manager of the St. James's Theatre, inspiration to Wilde and neighbor to Lillie Langtry. His long association with the St. James's began in 1890. Until Alexander took over, English playwrights had been ignored in favor of continental or Scandinavian writers like Ibsen. In contrast one of Alexander's first actions at the St. James's was to request a play from Wilde. Wilde offered him *The Duchess of Padua*. Alexander feared that the scenery would be too costly, so he asked Wilde to write on a more modern subject. The result was *Lady Windermere's Fan,* which Wilde wrote in less than three months.

For the opening night Wilde instructed some of his friends to buy green carnations at Goodyear's in the Royal Arcade, where he said they grew them. When they all arrived at the theatre with green carnations in their buttonholes, it provoked much curiosity, as Wilde had anticipated, until Wilde exposed the ploy by appearing for his curtain call wearing one himself. A typical "Wildeism."

Walk south from Pont Street and enter Cadogan Square.

5. Residence of Arthur James Balfour and Mary Elcho
62 Cadogan Square

Both members of the Souls' group of intelligencia, the couple who shared this large red-brick house was a prime example of the fact that the Souls had bodies. Although the Souls had an exalted opinion of their own mental gymnastic abilities, there were those who scoffed. One of them described Balfour as "the only quick mind in an ill-bred crowd."

Balfour's cold attitude toward friends' misfortunes was once explained as a defense against his own unstable emotions. As the resigned Mary once wrote to her lover, "You love me as much as a man can love a woman he has loved for ten years." To carry on an illicit affair in those days of Victorian morality demanded enormous diplomatic finesse.

Possibly Balfour's stature helped to preserve his reputation. A fellow Soul, Herbert Asquith, described him as having "an advantage over the rest of us insomuch as he is half a head higher than we are, both physically and intellectually."

In 1902 Balfour served for three years as prime minister and later, as foreign secretary, he drew up the Balfour Declaration, assuring British protection for the Jewish settlement of Palestine.

6. Residence of Arnold Bennett
75 Cadogan Square

This four-story red-brick house overlooking the elite square's lush, iron-gated park was where Bennett wrote most of his novels, even though his most famous were set in the "Five Towns" of the Midlands pottery district. He was greatly influenced by de Maupassant and specialized in sympathetic depiction of everyday life among the lower-middle classes. *The Old Wives' Tale* is best known today.

He was plagued with a stammer that was torture to him. One of his friends commented that had it not been for the stammer which forced him into introspection, Bennett might never have become a writer.

7. Residence of Lord Blandford
55-57 Cadogan Square

George Charles Spencer Churchill—Lord Blandford—was the eldest son of the Duke of Marlborough, brother to Randolph Churchill, and first in line to take over the title. He had been educated at Oxford, was an officer in the Horse Guards and was married to the daughter of the Duke of Aberdeen. Lord Blandford succeeded to his title in 1883 at a time when he was involved in one of the most scandalous and long-lasting trials of his century. And it was not even his first. Here was a man who could not escape trouble, nor women.

In 1878, while her husband was on a mission to India with the Prince of Wales, Lady Aylesford succumbed to an affair with the lascivious Blandford. Aylesford heard about it, hurried home, and came to a separation agreement with his wife, in which she promised not to see Blandford again. However before long they were staying together at the Hotel Rivoli in Paris as Mr. and Mrs. Spencer, whereupon Aylesford obtained a divorce. His former wife then faded into ignominious obscurity, while Lady Blandford forgave and forgot—momentarily.

In the bliss of reconciliation, the Blandfords purchased property and made plans for a new home to be built on this square, which was being developed by architect Norman Shaw for super-rich landowners who also owned country homes; hence there was no fenced resident's garden typical of most city squares. The Blandford home on the southeast corner was the most luxurious, with six windows facing the square on each of its five floors.

Perhaps all might have gone well had not an acquaintance of Blandford's, the enigmatic Lady Colin Campbell, been in the process of readying a new house for herself and her semi-invalid husband a short two blocks away on Cadogan Place. The two new home owners met, perhaps while posting letters at a corner mailbox. To quote a line from Wilde, Blandford's "aim in life was simply to be always looking for temptation." Characteristically he offered to inspect the work in progress at the beauteous lady's house. She, in turn, eagerly agreed to help him supervise his.

We shall leave the two neighbors now and pick them up again later at Lady Colin Campbell's house.

Return to Pont Street and turn right.

8. Residence of Lillie Langtry
21 Pont Street

Once her earning power as an actress was assured, Lillie Langtry acquired this towering, turreted, red terra-cotta house that so resembles a small castle, perhaps a subconscious manifestation of an unfulfilled wish.

Her stage career had enjoyed immediate success in London, and a year later American producers were begging for her. She arrived in New York in time to be met by Wilde, who was still there on his lecture tour and, like Wilde, she toured the entire country, performing at every major train stop. When she returned to England flushed with success, she moved into this Victorian confection and formed her own acting company, which toured the British Isles while she prepared for another prolonged U.S. tour.

Lillie Langtry's house on Pont Street.

Meanwhile Jeanne Marie, who called Lillie *ma tante,* was growing up. Accompanied by her guardian, Lillie's mother, she joined Lillie in America to travel in Lillie's private railroad car during her extensive second American tour. They were also accompanied by Freddie Gebhard, an American millionaire seriously in love with Lillie. The shadow of the drunken Edward Langtry still lurked in her background, however, and the threat he posed should he learn of her daughter. Lillie loved Freddie, but she couldn't risk marrying him.

In 1891, with Jeanne Marie at age ten, Lillie again returned to her Pont Street house in London. It was here that Wilde came to call with a play he had written for her. Its plot concerned a woman with a grown-up illegitimate daughter. Lillie was indignant at Wilde's allusion to the secret they shared. However she decided not to make an issue of his impertinence and instead retorted, "Now really, Oscar, do I look old enough to have a grown daughter of any description? Don't open the manuscript and don't read it to me. Put it away for twenty years." The play was *Lady Windermere's Fan*. Nothing to compare with it had been seen on the English stage since Sheridan's *The School for Scandal* over a century earlier. It brought Wilde fame and money, but it wreaked havoc with an old friendship.

Lillie had never been enthralled with theater; for her the stage was simply a means to an end. On her tours to the West in America, she had bought land near Carson City, Nevada upon which silver was discovered. In Salt Lake City, Utah, where she was fascinated with the Mormons' history of polygamy, she purchased land her agent later sold for a forty-thousand-dollar profit. In rapidly growing Chicago she enjoyed another fruitful real-estate venture. In addition to her lucrative investments, her acting company was hugely profitable.

Lillie now returned to London to live permanently. Financially secure, she could retire from the stage and devote her full attention to a new pursuit —the acquisition of a stable of fine racing horses, an interest she shared with her old friend and lover, the Prince of Wales. Because it wasn't quite acceptable for an independent woman to be active in the racing world, she ran her horses under the name of Mr. Jersey. When her famous horse, Merman, won England's most important long-distance handicap, the Cesarewitch, on her forty-fourth birthday, the Prince of Wales escorted her into the sacrosanct Jockey Club enclosure—the first woman ever allowed in there.

In 1899 Lillie's estranged husband, whom she supported with an annual allowance on condition he stay away from her, died of alcoholism. At last Lillie was free to remarry. Her romance with the American Freddie Gebhard had ended. Louis Battenberg, Jeanne Marie's father, had already made a family-approved marriage, and Lillie's most recent lover (who had contributed to her stable) had suddenly died. Considering all of the men who now courted her, she married the most unlikely—Sir Hugo de Bathe, a bon vivant nineteen years her junior with little wit, but great physical appeal. Moreover he stood in line for a title. At last Lillie could become a lady!

Turn right off Pont Street into Cadogan Place.

9. The Cadogan Hotel
75 Cadogan Place

This charming Belgravia hotel, still popular with discerning travelers, stands hardly a block removed from Lillie's Pont Street house. It was in a room here that Oscar Wilde was arrested with his lover, Lord Alfred Douglas, whom he called "Bosie." The unfortunate episode inspired a poem by nineteenth-century journalist John Betjeman that pretty well tells the story the way it happened:

Wilde's friends, Reggie Turner and Robbie Ross, were with him—

When the knock came on the door.
He sipped a weak hock and seltzer
As he gazed at the London skies
Through the Nottingham lace of the curtains
Or was it his bees-winged eyes?
To the right and before him Pont Street
Did tower in her new built red,
As hard as the morning gaslight
That shown on his unmade bed
"I want some more hock in my seltzer
And, Robbie, please give me your hand—
Is this the end or the beginning?
How can I understand?
"So you've brought me the latest The Yellow Book
And Buchan has got in it now;
Approval of what is approved of
Is as false as a well-kept vow.
"One astrakhan coat is at Willie's—
Another one's at the Savoy,
Do fetch my morocco portmanteau,
And bring them on later, dear boy."
A thump, and a murmur of voices—
(Oh, why must they make such a din?)
As the door of the bedroom swung open
And TWO PLAINCLOTHES POLICEMEN came in;
"Mr. Woilde, we 'ave come for tew take yew
Where felons and criminals dwell:
We must ask yew tew leave with us quietly
For this is the Cadogan Hotel."

He rose, and he put down The Yellow Book.
He staggered—and, terrible-eyed,
He brushed past the palms on the staircase
And was helped to a hansom outside.

The police did permit Wilde to leave a note for Douglas, who at the time of his arrest was on an errand. The note requested him to contact friends for bail and to ask a barrister to call on Wilde at the Bow Street Police Court.

The Cadogan Hotel, where Wilde was arrested.

The exposure and the trial that ensued came about largely as a personal vendetta on the part of the ninth Marquess of Queensberry, when he suspected that his son, Lord Alfred Douglas, already a known pederast, was involved with Wilde. Wilde had opportunities to escape to France, and was urged by solicitors and friends to do so, but he insisted upon seeing the case through to the end. It was an unpleasant episode on all counts—as much in relation to the laws of the time, the outdated cultural mores of the era, and the vindictive rage of an unbalanced personality, as on the part of the apologetic defendant, who once explained himself thus: "Tired of being on the heights, I deliberately went to the depths in search of a new sensation."

10. Residence of Sir Charles Dilke and Sir Herbert Tree
76 Sloane Street

A politician with a lightning brain, Sir Charles Dilke cultivated both the Marlborough set and the artists. He was a republican-minded radical of the Liberal party, and many considered this lucid humanitarian to be the obvious successor to Gladstone.

In 1881, while under secretary for foreign affairs, Dilke attempted to negotiate with the queen to effect some minor participation in government by the Prince of Wales, but the queen, hinting that she "deprecated the discussion of national secrets over country-house dinner tables," refused to give any responsibility to her lively son and heir.

Sir Herbert Beerbohm Tree, the actor and theatre manager whom we met on the St. James's walk, was the half brother of the notorious *Punch* writer, Sir Max Beerbohm. Tree successfully managed the Haymarket Theatre some ten years before building the imposing Her Majesty's Theatre

Sir Herbert Beerbohm Tree.

111

across the street from the Haymarket. He liked playing character parts and was praised as a hilarious Joseph in Sheridan's *The School for Scandal,* in which he performed with Lillie Langtry playing Lady Teazle—a professional replay of her performance in the part many years earlier.

In an interview after Wilde's death, Tree said, "Oscar was the greatest man I have ever known—and the greatest gentleman." As Tree knew pretty well every notable of his time, his tribute is not without significance.

Sloane Street runs along the west side of Cadogan Place, forming a square which was developed in 1877 as London's first big square. Its two iron-gated gardens offered a peaceful, prestigious woodland setting for its illustrious residents. The grand mansions on its north end have been replaced by the Carlton House Hotel, but the five-story mansions with white pillars, Tuscan porticoes and iron balconies on the east side are much as they were in 1881, when Lady Colin Campbell moved into the neighborhood. Other residents then included the Marchioness of Queensberry (Lord Douglas's mother), General Henry James Barre, the Lord Bishop of Derry, Admirals Sir A. L. Montgomery and George Willes, and Lord Bromwell, to name just a few. All of the then single-family dwellings contained the usual servants' quarters below the stairs and five floors above ground with fourteen rooms.

11. Site of Last London Residence of Lillie Langtry
Cadogan Place (now the Carlton House Hotel)

After the wedding the new Lady de Bathe and her husband, whom she called "Shuggy," moved into a grand mansion at this address, not far from her old Pont Street home. She filled the new house with racing trophies from her winning horses, a fine collection of silver and old china, and rare period furniture. The big conversation piece was Rameses, a great grizzly bear from the Rockies weighing a thousand pounds, which had been shot by her brother on a visit to the American West. Now it stood erect, some seven feet high, in her wide entrance hall, scaring people with its lifelike appearance. Lillie loved being photographed clutching one of its huge paws. She considered the trophy a good-luck charm and carried it in a special trunk on all of her trips to America.

Her boudoir had several walls lined with a continuous wardrobe featuring hundreds of dresses. The bathroom walls were turquoise-and-blue mosaic with starlike glints of gold, and her tub was marble. Off the dining room was a formal room with a minstrel gallery, where a small orchestra played for dinners. She had one of the first telephones in London, and a ticker tape to give her the results of various race meetings on which she had placed bets.

She lived here until her retirement to the south of France in 1919.

Lillie Langtry.

12. Residence of Lady Colin Campbell
79 Cadogan Place

On November 26, 1886 began the longest, most sensational divorce trial in British history, *Campbell v. Campbell*. Lady Colin charged her husband with cruelty, while he accused her of having sex with a duke (her neighbor, Blandford), a general (William Butler), a surgeon (Tom Bird), and London's fire chief (Captain Shaw).

Both parties had grounds. Following a lengthy engagement, Lord Colin had entered into marriage in July of 1881 with an innocent girl, telling her that they would not be able to live as man and wife until his doctor advised him that it would be safe. He did not admit to her, nor to her suspicious father, that the mysterious ailment for which he was under treatment was an advanced case of syphilis. A nurse lived with them, and even accompanied them on their honeymoon. When some months later, under Lord Colin's doctor's advice, Lady Colin finally lost her virginity, it was an unpleasant experience. As a result she acquired an infection, although one of a different nature from her husband's.

Meanwhile Lord Colin suffered a relapse. Discouraged with his progress, he engaged a new surgeon, Tom Bird, who also treated Lady Colin during her illness. Bird was no more immune to her charms than was a family friend, Captain Shaw, who came to pay his respects to the new home owners.

Fully recovered, Lady Colin carried on a lively social life, often receiving her new neighbor, Lord Blandford, or Captain Shaw in the drawing room, while Lord Colin remained bedridden upstairs. This lady was more than just a social butterfly. She was talented, creative and brilliant at a time when women were not supposed to be talented, creative and brilliant. She had traveled widely with her parents, she had written a number of published articles, she was an accomplished vocalist who gave recitals for charity, and her paintings had been exhibited. (It was while she was studying painting with General Butler's artist wife that he fell victim to her charms.) She was beautiful, rode and swam well, and kept herself informed. Whatever she did, she did well.

So well, in fact, that Lord Colin's nurses and some of the servants started to suspect that her prowess was being exercised in the drawing room downstairs. This, of course, led to whispers which ultimately precipitated the lawsuits. During the trial reports from former servants, hansom-cab drivers and nurses reiterated that numerous clandestine visits had been made to her drawing room by the above-mentioned gentlemen, whom Lord Colin brought to trial. Due to his reputation as a rake established in the earlier Aylesford case, Blandford's name was preeminent. When he was asked during cross-examination why he had so often sought Lady Colin's company, the jury could hardly suppress its mirth when Blandford answered "her conversation."

The physician Bird also inspired incredulity when he explained that his visits to Lady Colin's boudoir had been conducted in the process of treatment. But most dramatic of all was the courtroom testimony of what a butler whom Lady Colin had previously fired had seen while peeping through the drawing-room keyhole. He had witnessed Lady Colin and Captain Shaw lying on the carpet.

"Did you see Lady Colin's face and head?" Lord Colin's attorney asked the butler in the witness box.

"Yes," answered the butler.

"And her feet?"

"No, I could not see them. They were toward the door."

"Did you see her bust?"

"I certainly saw more than that."

"What did you see of Captain Shaw?"

"He was over her, and I saw his head and body."

"How low down?"

"To the waist."

What a sensation! Lady Colin had actually been caught in the act by a witness!

Both she and Shaw denied the accusation during their turns on the stand, but their case looked dire until her brilliant barrister cross-examined the butler.

"Is it not a fact that if there is no key in the keyhole, on each side of the door a brass covering falls down?" the butler was asked.

"I guess you know. I don't," the butler responded.

"Do you not know that if there is no key in the door, the coverings fall down on both sides of the door?" the barrister persisted.

"I don't remember."

"And don't you know that it is the pressure of the key that keeps the covering up? And that if the key is in one side of the door, the covering will fall down on the other side?"

"Yes."

"Do you persist in swearing that you could see through the keyhole?"

"Not that I could, but that I did," the butler proclaimed.

Judge Butt, who himself lived on Cadogan Place in an identical house a few removed from the Colin Campbells, was convinced of what the jurors would find when they took the unprecedented step of visiting Lady Colin's house to look through the now-celebrated keyhole. They returned with the announcement that what they had found discredited the evidence of one of the witnesses. "Of course you mean the butler," the judge concluded.

"On the contrary," the spokesman responded, rendering the judge dumbstruck. After a few seconds of stunned silence, the judge directed the foreman to deliver his report.

*Lady Colin Campbell (courtesy of
the National Portrait Gallery, London).*

The foreman rose. "We find the escutcheons of the keyhole are very stiff and will stay up at right angles, and we found it impossible to put the outside escutcheon in a perpendicular position at all."

The case went on for weeks with charges and countercharges. It ended with a hopelessly deadlocked jury. Whether Lady Colin had committed adultery beyond a doubt with all or none of the men appeared impossible to determine. After a second consideration the jury finally concluded that, since they couldn't prove that she was guilty, she was not. Lord Colin, on the other hand, was guilty of jeopardizing her health and not being honest in regard to his condition when they had married. He was forced to pay the legal fees, and her divorce was granted. His father paid the costs. Lord Colin disappeared to Bombay to practice law and died at age forty-two.

Although the stigma of this affair stuck to Lady Colin Campbell for the rest of her life, she enjoyed a successful writing career. In addition to several novels and a play, she wrote a weekly column under the pen name of Vera Tsaritsyn called "A Woman's Walk," that contained essays on places at home and abroad which she had visited—travel literature at its best.

Lord Blandford escaped the vengeance of the court, but not that of his wife. Soon he was in court anew, this time being sued for divorce—thus proving again Wilde's lines from *Dorian Gray:* "Those who are unfaithful know the pleasures of love; it is the faithful who know love's tragedies." Blandford remarried in 1888 and died four years later of a heart attack.

From Cadogan Place cut over to the north end of Eaton Terrace.

13. Duke of Wellington Pub and Nicholson's Wine Bar
63 Eaton Terrace

The wine bar, where lunch is served, is upstairs above the pub, overlooking charming Eaton Mews across the street. Both the pub and wine bar are attractive, cozy and friendly, with paneled walls and rafters hung with horse brasses. The food is good pub fare—lamb casseroles and cottage pies. Sandwiches on crusty bread, heaped with thinly sliced roast beef or a selection of cheeses, are also good.

The street at the corner leads into Eaton Square. At the turn of the century, the dignified Georgian mansions on this lushly gardened square attracted an imposing population of the peerage—Lord Chelmsford at number 7, Lord Hampton at number 9, the Marchioness of Headfort at number 11, to say nothing of Lord Beresford at number 100. In addition to the above, Eaton Square housed seventeen dukes, earls and viscounts; eight knights, one foreign count, nine titled ladies, a trio of admirals, the same number of generals, and nine members of Parliament. To live here called for an income of at least ten thousand pounds a year, ten servants and a first-class cook.

14. Residence of Lord Charles Beresford and Nancy Astor
100 Eaton Square

A celebrated lover, dashing admiral and sometime friend of the Prince of Wales, Beresford's amorous adventures were prone to surprise endings. One of his romps occurred at a country-house party. The hostess had sagely billeted certain married couples in separate bedrooms conveniently far apart, but had neglected to provide a room plan. During the evening's festivities Lord Charles surreptitiously arranged a midnight assignation with a lovely lady, rumored to be Lady Gladys de Grey. At the appropriate time, exalted over having successfully sneaked unseen down the hall, he burst into the lady's chamber and leaped into her bed crowing, "Cock-a-doodle-doo!" When trembling hands finally got the paraffin lamp going, he found himself deposited between the Bishop of Chester and his wife.

Ever prone to frustrations in his love life, the dashing Lord Charles found himself at a later date embroiled in a legal hassle when his wife intercepted a letter from one of his more serious inamoratas, whom he recently had deserted. This lady, the Countess of Warwick, called Daisy, had exasperated him by indiscreetly marching into his wife's room at another country-house party and recklessly announcing her intention of eloping with him—an act which had resulted in Lady Beresford immediately packing him up and taking him home. This had proved a wise move on her part, since after the exposure, Beresford had lost interest in the illicit romance.

The lady, on the other hand, had not. A renowned beauty, Lady Daisy was not accustomed to being spurned. When she heard a few months later that Lady Beresford was pregnant, her anger turned to rage; she was infuriated that her lover had jilted her for, of all people, his wife! Daisy wrote him a blistering letter, asserting that he had fathered one of her children and demanding that he leave his wife and join her on the Riviera. This was the letter Lady Beresford intercepted and sagely delivered to George Lewis, an attorney who had a monopoly on cases where the sins and follies of aristocrats threatened exposure.

Lord Charles Beresford as seen in Vanity Fair, *August 12, 1876.*

Lewis immediately sent Daisy a warning. Any further annoyance to his client on her part would result in actions detrimental to her. Alarmed over this unexpected turn of events, Daisy demanded the return of her letter. Lewis refused on grounds that the letter was now legally the property of Lord Charles Beresford.

Incensed that her hated rival might in the future threaten her with the letter, Daisy then turned to the Prince of Wales, a close friend of Beresford's, knowing that Bertie would do anything to avoid a scandal involving a member of his set. Bertie also would do almost anything to comfort a lady in distress. As Daisy later wrote in her memoirs, "He was more than kind, and suddenly I saw him looking at me in a way all women understand."

Within weeks Daisy's influence with the prince became evident. Lady Beresford found herself banned from Marlborough House social functions. Spurred on by his slighted wife, Lord Charles called on the prince. Harsh words passed between the erstwhile friends, which resulted in Lord Charles suddenly receiving orders to take command of a ship destined for foreign ports. By this time the Prince of Wales was deeply immersed in a serious love affair with the distressed Lady Daisy.

The Beresfords were not through yet, however. To accommodate his nagging wife, Lord Charles dispatched a letter to Prime Minister Salisbury threatening public exposure of all sorts of princely peccadilloes, as well as Daisy's letter, if his wife was not reinstated socially with a public apology from the prince. He also demanded that Daisy be ostracized.

There followed days of negotiations so frantic that Lord Beresford returned from overseas and Queen Victoria became involved. Lord Salisbury finally effected a settlement. For a brief period Daisy was restricted to entertaining the prince privately on her own Easton Lodge estate.

With peace once again restored, Daisy became the prince's second officially recognized mistress, following Lillie Langtry, until she eventually overstepped her bounds and made way for the bridge-playing Alice Keppel. Beresford, meanwhile, continued to prove Wilde's premise that "experience is the name everyone gives to their mistakes."

Many years later in 1958, Lady Nancy Astor, the first woman member of the House of Commons (whom we met on the St. James's walk) retired to 100 Eaton Square. By then it was a flat, but enormous, formed by the first floor of number 100, as well as that of the next house and the one after it. "I don't like having to live in an apartment," she complained, however. "What's my butler got to do without his own front door? I see people coming in at the door from the street or meet them on the stairs and I have no notion who they are, but can't ask them, 'Who are you?' I believe some are even Italians!"

Turn right at the end of Eaton Square onto Belgrave Place and follow it in an easterly direction to Chester Square.

15. Residence of Sarah Bernhardt
77 Chester Square

Sarah Bernhardt lived in this charming house tucked into the corner of the square when she came to London for her first appearance at the Gaiety Theatre. She was amazed upon her arrival to find invitations from titled individuals awaiting her, since in France at that time, theatre people were not socially accepted by the upper crust. Later she learned that her old friend, Marshal Canrobert, a former diplomat, had written to Lord Dudley asking him and his wife to look out for the young artist. Lady Dudley, lively and witty herself, considered it rather a lark to introduce Sarah to the Marlborough set, especially since the Prince of Wales, who had seen Bernhardt perform with the Comédie Française, had asked her and her neighbors, the Rothschilds, to extend their hospitality to her. The aristocrats appeared on demand, but remained aloof. Bernhardt, indifferent to their snubs, preferred to spend her time with Wilde and his arty friends anyway.

After witnessing the divine Sarah's performance, her neighbor, Matthew Arnold, declared her "a fugitive vision of delicate features under a shower of hair and a cloud of lace," while Ellen Terry wrote, "She was as transparent as an azalea only more so; like a cloud only not so thick; smoke from a burning paper describes her more nearly."

Needless to say Bernhardt was a greater hit in the theatre than in the drawing room. A dowager, upon hearing Bernhardt speak of her son, said, "Why, I didn't know you were married."

"I am not, Madame la Comtesse," Bernhardt answered sweetly, "My son was *un petit accident d'amour.*"

Neighbors on Chester Square next to the private garden adjacent to Bernhardt's house complained of her "zoo." She kept four dogs, a parrot named Bizibouzon, and a caged monkey called Darwin. She also traveled with seven chameleons, which she wore one at a time, attached to a gold chain, to match her gown.

Bernhardt was well received by London's theatre audience and returned for future appearances until she

The Divine Sarah Bernhardt.

became disenchanted with Victorian restrictions, such as the fiasco when she attempted to produce Wilde's *Salomé* at the Palace Theatre.

16. Residence of Matthew Arnold
2 Chester Square

On a cold day in February 1858, Arnold wrote, "We have taken a house in Chester Square. It is a very small one, but it will be something to unpack one's portmanteau for the first time since I was married, now nearly seven years ago." The Arnolds remained here for ten years, during which time he was recognized as one of the leading poets and humanists of his day.

In spite of the philosophical differences between the brilliant scientist Thomas Huxley, who publicly defended Darwin against the clergy, and the scholarly Arnold, who advanced the importance of a classical education as opposed to a scientific one, the two men were friendly rivals. Arnold eventually sacrificed poetry in favor of lecturing on education, both in England and America. Wilde had been greatly influenced by his lectures when Arnold was professor of poetry at Oxford.

17. Residence of Mary Wollstonecraft Shelley
24 Chester Square

Mrs. Shelley, widow of the poet Percy Bysshe Shelley, died here in 1851. After running away with Shelley in 1814, she married him two years later. While they lived in Italy, she wrote *Frankenstein.* Although Wilde at one time referred to her famous husband as a boy's poet, engraved over the doorway on a heavy beam in his Chelsea house, he had the following lines from Shelley inscribed in gilt, red and blue:

> *Spirit of Beauty! Tarry still awhile,*
> *They are not dead, thine ancient votaries.*
> *Some few there are to whom thy radiant smile*
> *Is better than a thousand victories.*

Ebury Street, where George Moore lived, runs perpendicular to the end of Belgrave Place, south of Chester Square, but is not in a particularly interesting neighborhood. Instead we suggest that you return to Eaton Square and follow Belgrave Place northwest to Belgrave Square.

18. Residence of George Moore
121 Ebury Street

Of Moore's novels, *Esther Waters,* influenced by Émile Zola, was the most popular, although in Wilde's view, "He leads his readers to the latrine and locks them in." The plot is an exposé of the Victorian attitude to illegitimacy among the working class and the existence of "baby" farms.

For a short period Moore was the center of London literary life and gossip, and his various love affairs were well publicized, especially by himself. One lady complained, "Some men kiss and do not tell; some kiss and tell, but George Moore told and did not kiss."

Another contemporary wrote, "George was licentious in mind and collected photographs of his women adorers, and told racy little anecdotes with the idea of appearing more of a rake than he was. I think he was really an old monk, living in the wrong century, and it pleased him to play the rake."

It has been said that the Irish dislike one another with fervor, which might have accounted for the antipathy that existed between Moore and Wilde. On the other hand Moore was mean in his habits, coarse in his language, and narrow in his interests. Wilde was generous, refined in language and had broad interests. Moore acquired his style painfully; Wilde's came by instinct. Once when asked if he knew Moore, Wilde answered, "I know him so well that I haven't spoken to him for ten years."

Follow Belgrave Place westward to Belgrave Square, one of the most impressive in London, with opulent mansions angled across its corners, giving the effect of a stately circle around an immense garden centerpiece.

19. Residence of Reuben Sassoon
1 Belgrave Square

Reuben was the first member of the Sassoon family (called the "Rothschilds of the East") to arrive in London. He came in 1858; others followed. Within a few years the family boasted two baronets and was sending its sons to Eton and Oxford. Silver, gold, silks, spices, gums, opium, cotton, wool and wheat—whatever moved over land and sea felt the hand and bore the mark of the Sassoons from Bombay.

Reuben Sassoon gave up his first mansion in Lancaster Gate and built this even grander one in Belgravia on the corner of Belgrave Square and Wilton Crescent. The house was so oddly constructed that his carriage and horses had to be carried up by lift to stables on the roof. You can still see the iron fence that contained them. The house also boasted a spacious conservatory for exotic plants. Sassoon frequently entertained the Prince of Wales and kept a good, spicy, oriental table. He selected only the finest of pink champagne, which the prince was making fashionable at that time.

Reuben had an unattractive wife who disappeared when his sporting friends came to call, so although he played cards at the Marlborough Club, he was not quite one of the Marlborough social set. He was, however, a great friend of the Prince of Wales and accompanied him on his annual pilgrimage to Marienbad, an Austrian spa where they went to lose weight. One memorable year they were entertained there by Maud Allen, who danced for them wearing only two oyster shells and a tantalizing five-franc piece (the same Maud Allen whom Margot Tennant Asquith later brought to dance at number 10 Downing Street).

20. Residence of the Earl of Shaftesbury
5 Belgrave Square

Among the embassies on the square is the former home of the philanthropic Earl of Shaftesbury (the one honored by Eros on Piccadilly Circus). He died here in 1885. It was this gentleman who made rescuing fallen women fashionable. Cartoons of the time often depicted ladies in prim bonnets, armed with tracts and stout umbrellas, pursuing prostitutes through the streets. The purpose of the umbrella was to ward off pimps while the well-meaning ladies begged the unfortunates to repent and enter "homes of hope" founded by Lord Shaftesbury. Even Gladstone was an enthusiastic worker for this cause, at some cost to his reputation. There were those who unjustly believed that his preoccupation with prostitutes was not a wholly disinterested one.

Follow Wilton Crescent to Wilton Place, and then the short distance north to Knightsbridge. There, on the north side of the street adjacent to Hyde Park at Albert's Gate, stand two grand white mansions. The one on your left is number 2.

21. Residence of Arthur Sassoon
2 Albert Gate

Arthur Sassoon, Reuben's brother, married Louise Perugia, a young niece of the Rothschilds whom he had met in Vienna on a tour of Europe. When they moved into this majestic house overlooking Hyde Park's Rotten Row, the elegant Louise decorated it in the French manner with brocade upholstery and white painted walls. Margot Tennant, a wheel in London society who later married Prime Minister Asquith, praised Louise as "one of the most tasteful women I've ever known." Among Louise's guests were such socialites as the Duchess of Devonshire, Millie Sutherland and Lady de Grey. It is said that her white-gloved footmen were even taller than those of the Rothschilds, where wages were reputedly scaled by the inch.

Louise and her friend, Hannah Rosebery (a Rothschild), went in for matchmaking. Hannah's cousin, Leopold de

Rothschild, immensely rich with several estates and a mansion at 5 Hamilton Place in Mayfair, had everything except a wife. Louise had a younger sister. Leopold had always said that he would never marry until he found someone as beautiful and accomplished as Louise Sassoon, so they produced her sister Maria, who was on a visit from Italy. Leopold was fanatically interested in horses. Maria didn't ride. But the girls coaxed her into taking lessons, and one day introduced her to Leopold at a meet. He was predictably fascinated, and soon they were wed in the Central Synagogue in Great Portland Street, with the Prince of Wales and Disraeli both attending. Among the newlyweds' treasures was a letter from Disraeli congratulating the bridegroom on his choice and confessing, "I have always been of the opinion that there cannot be too many Rothschilds." (They produced three.)

22. Rotten Row
Hyde Park

Extending alongside Knightsbridge on the south side of Hyde Park runs the bridle path known affectionately to Londoners as Rotten Row. Its name is a derivation of *route du roi,* taken from the time when King George II lived in Kensington Palace and took this route to and from Whitehall. It was along this sand track that the notorious Skittles made her first inroads into society. And it was here that London

Horsemanship on display at route du rois, *or "Rotten Row" in Hyde Park.*

newcomers Lillie Langtry and Oscar Wilde strolled together and plotted their entrées into the social whirl.

The scene that impressed Lillie most when she came to London was the exciting spectacle of Rotten Row between twelve and two, when fashionable society congregated here to ride, drive, walk, see, and be seen. Everyone dressed to the teeth: women in the latest mode, and men in frock coats, pearl gray trousers, varnished boots and, of course, top hats. For two hours the crowds pushed and jostled slowly up and down each side of the Row, bowing and smiling, and watching the four-in-hand coaches, pony carriages, tilburies, broughams and dignified barouches with handsome, high-stepping grays, blacks or whites; their coachmen and footmen rigid in flashing livery.

Rotten Row was also a showcase for outstanding horsemanship. When one of her admirers, Moreton Frewen, presented Lillie Langtry with a fine horse named Redskin, she could match the best, having acquired riding skill as a girl in Jersey. Later, crowds in the park used to trample one another just to catch a glimpse of the famous beauty, mistress to the king.

Busses passing along Knightsbridge connect with transportation in most directions, which will carry you to your destination.

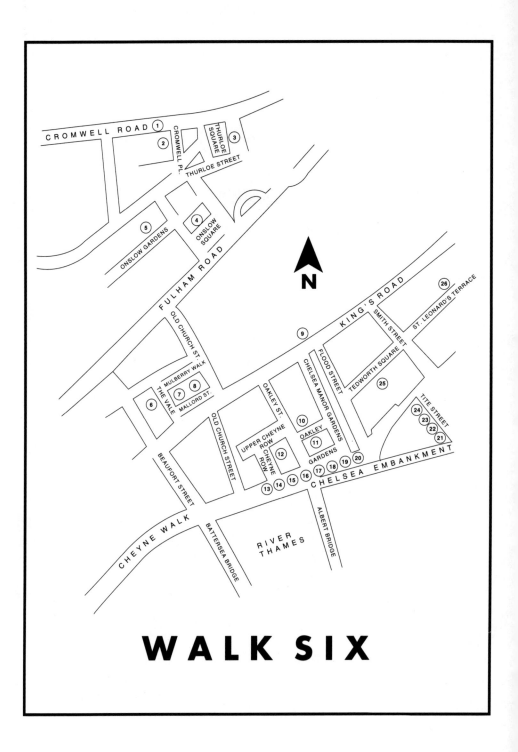

WALK SIX

Ever since 1874, when the embankment was completed that removed forever the mud flats, tree-shaded shoreline and country lanes of this bankside community along the Thames, Chelsea has been populated by artists, writers and those of a bohemian bent. It is not primarily a residential district of stately houses, but rather one of nineteenth- and twentieth-century terrace houses, cottages and flats, with bustling streets filled with antique shops and boutiques crowded in between.

Cromwell Road and Cromwell Place

Our walk begins on the north border of Chelsea, across from the Victoria and Albert Museum, where the bus stops on the corner of Cromwell Road and Cromwell Place.

1. Residence of Sir Charles James Freake
21 Cromwell Road

This fine corner house, which is now the French Consulate, was the home of a builder and patron of the arts called "the cleverest of all the speculating builders" of his time. Freake was not clever enough, however, to make Lillie Langtry receptive to the Prince of Wales's first seduction attempt at an amorous assignation in his house.

Freake lived in the imposing residence he had built in 1860 with his wife and daughter, three female relations, a butler, two footmen and seven other servants. By arranging nefarious financial favors, he had managed to obtain the patronage of the Prince of Wales, who sometimes attended musical and theatrical performances staged in the great ballroom of the house.

After the prince had been introduced to Lillie, she was astonished a short time later to be taken aside by the heavy-handed Mr. Freake and informed that the prince was interested in paying his respects to her in the privacy of the Freake mansion. The date was set and the appointment kept, but unlike other ladies summoned by the prince, Lillie cunningly postponed the actual seduction, allowing time for the prince to become acquainted with her more enduring charms. This ingenious strategy may have been responsible for her ascension to the position of his first officially recognized royal mistress.

The son of a coal merchant and publican, Freake was granted a baronetcy in 1882, some years after he had built, at his own cost, the National Training School for Music (now the Royal College of Organists) in 1875 and made his mansion available for other princely assignations. The prince was particularly interested in the school and, according to Gladstone's political secretary, had "persistently and somewhat questionably [if not fishily] pressed Freake's name on the prime minister"; hence the reward of the title.

2. Residence of Sir John Everett Millais
7 Cromwell Place

This artist, who ranks among England's greatest, lived here early in his career, while he was struggling for recognition, along with fellow Pre-Raphaelites Dante Gabriel Rossetti and William Holman Hunt. When Millais learned that he could do better by painting in a more popular mode, he quietly drifted away from his colleagues' philosophical approach and produced the kind of paintings the public wanted to see. It paid off handsomely. He soon built a much grander abode in Kensington. We shall pick up his story again there.

At the south end of Cromwell Place, turn into Thurloe Square, a short block to the east on Thurloe Street.

3. Residence of the Edmund Maghlin Blood Family
46 Thurloe Square

It was when she lived in this house with her parents, the Bloods, that their daughter Gertrude became engaged to marry Lord Colin Campbell. Although a well-respected family, the Bloods lived a relatively quiet life and were not household names in London until the notorious divorce trial of their daughter, after she had become Lady Colin Campbell (which we heard about on the Belgravia walk). Lord Colin had postponed the wedding twice due to health problems, and then finally demanded a prenuptial agreement, stating that Gertrude would be prepared to nurse him until his doctor gave permission to consummate the marriage. The Bloods had every reason to suspect foul play. Still, when Gertrude's father asked Lord Colin point-blank if he had that "loathsome" disease, he claimed it was only a fistula. In Victorian times such delicate matters were not discussed.

Gertrude was eager for the marriage, and her mother no less so, possibly because it presented an opportunity for her daughter to move into the aristocracy. Lord Colin's father, the Duke of Argyll, plainly opposed the match, wishing a more auspicious mate for his son and heir. The marriage appeared doomed from the start. Nevertheless the Bloods stood by their daughter throughout the trial and lived in seclusion when it was over.

You will notice windows which have been bricked in on the exposed side of this corner house, as well as on others. This resulted from a "window tax" once levied on home owners. To reduce taxes, residents blocked in unnecessary windows. Later, when the tax was removed, many preferred the interior wall space to windows, and left them blocked. Retrace your steps to Cromwell Place and proceed south to Onslow Square.

4. Residence of William Makepeace Thackeray
36 Onslow Square

After his children were teenagers, the famous novelist moved to this charming square with its Georgian houses

William Makepeace Thackery.

graced by white-columned porticoes supporting balconies. It was here that he completed his classic novel, *The Virginians*. The dramatic stone steeple of St. Paul's Onslow Square Church creates a striking focal point for the lovely garden around which the square is built.

In 1862 Thackeray's health was failing and he moved back to Kensington. We shall visit an earlier house he had built and learn more about his life on the Kensington walk.

Pass through Onslow Square to Onslow Gardens.

5. Residence of James Anthony Froude
5 Onslow Gardens

Historian and man of letters, Froude met Thomas Carlyle in 1849 and became a frequent visitor to his Chelsea home. He shared Carlyle's ideas. "If I wrote anything," he confessed, "I fancied myself writing to him, reflecting at each word on what he would think of it as a check on affectations." He was Carlyle's literary executor and wrote a full and frank biography of him. His reputation as one of the great masters of English prose in the nineteenth century was established with the publication of his twelve-volume *A History of England from the Fall of Wolsey to the Death of Elizabeth*. This work brought him to the attention of London society and until his death in 1894, he made his home at Onslow Gardens.

Now walk south on Old Church Street, which extends from the center of Onslow Gardens, and follow it to Mulberry Walk. En route, at 125 Old Church Street, you will pass a charming house with a large front studio, built at the turn of the century by ceramist William de Morgan and his artist-wife Evelyn. Some of his rich tiles enhance the fanciful Leighton House museum we shall visit on the Kensington walk.

Turn right off Old Church Street onto Mulberry Walk, a short, charming thoroughfare of cottage-type houses with leaded window muntins and little gardens. Note the interesting old sundial atop the Victorian house at number 23. Then turn left onto The Vale.

6. Residence of James A. McNeill Whistler
The Vale

For a short time around 1885, Whistler took a place here before moving to Cheyne Walk. The Vale is "an amazing place," he said. "You might be in the heart of the country, and there, two steps away, is the King's Road. Mine is the first on the right after you go through the iron gates."

It was part of Whistler's policy at this time to keep himself in the public eye, so many things were written about the Vale house and his friends. A description in the *Court and Society Review* on July 1, 1886 describes the house with plain whitewashed walls and unadorned wooden rafters, which partly form a loft for the stowing of canvases, pastels, etcetera: "Vast space is unencumbered by furniture and a large table-palate gives the appearance of a serious working place. Whistler paints in a velvet coat and embroidered smoking cap or black clothes of his ordinary wear, straight from the street to his easel."

In his studio in The Vale, Whistler painted a full-length portrait of Walter Sickert, a favorite pupil and one of his cleverest disciples. He also painted several portraits of Mrs. Godwin, the wife of the architect who had designed his beloved "White House," whom he was destined to marry in August 1888, a little over a year following her husband's death.

It was after his marriage, and to escape lingering memories of Maud, a former model and mistress, that Whistler and his bride left The Vale and moved to Tower House on Tite Street. The new place was in such disorder from the hasty marriage and move that he ordered the wedding breakfast sent in from the Café Royal.

Walk a short distance along The Vale and then turn left (east) onto Mallord Street, another "old English" atmospheric street, with colorful window boxes and individually designed, freestanding houses.

7. Residence of Augustus John
24 Mallord Street

This colorful Welsh artist is celebrated today for his portraits of notable people, among them Bernard Shaw and Thomas Hardy. Resembling a great and grand figure from the Old Testament, he was a popular character around Chelsea and liked by Wilde. Considered a "bohemian," he lusted and drank to excess, but was careful never to use profanity. A number of the portraits he painted now hang in the National Portrait Gallery.

John also resided for a time at 33 Tite Street.

8. Residence of A.A. Milne
13 Mallord Street

This red-brick house, with its curlicue wrought-iron fence, flagstone entrance and leaded windows, is what one might expect to find as the residence of the author of *Winnie-the-Pooh*. Milne took up free-lance journalism after obtaining a degree at Cambridge. His light, witty style was at home in the pages of *Punch*, and in 1906 he became assistant editor. The stage comedies he wrote in 1920 and 1921—*Mr. Pim Passes By* and *The Truth about Gladys Blayds*—established his reputation, although he was always peevish that critics didn't regard him as a heavyweight. His son Christopher Robin inspired the world of *Winnie-the-Pooh* and its sequels.

Probably the best line Milne ever came up with occurred on his deathbed, when he observed, "My exit is the result of too many entrées."

Turn right to King's Road and follow it in an eastward direction. This street acquired its name when it was a private royal way from Hampton Court to St. James's until 1801.

9. Residence of Ellen Terry and James Carew
215 Kings Road

In 1902 Ellen Terry moved from South Kensington to Chelsea, but unhappiness followed her here. She had finished her last provincial tour with Henry Irving and had begun acting with her own company, assisted by her son Teddy, until he suddenly disappeared. When she next heard from him, he was in Germany and in love with Isadora Duncan, the eccentric originator of modern dance, whose life ended so dramatically in the south of France when her long scarf got caught in the wheels of an open car and choked her to death.

Teddy was married when he met Isadora Duncan, so the relationship was doomed from the start. They had a daughter, Deidre, born after Teddy had returned to his wife in London for the birth of their son. Isadora never stopped suffering over her loss of Teddy and wrote disturbing letters to Ellen. Compounding Ellen's distress over the situation, her granddaughter's life ended tragically while she was still an infant. She was riding in a car in Paris with her half brother Patrick when the car plunged out of control into the Seine. They both drowned.

Dame Alice Ellen Terry, painted in 1876 by J. Forbes-Robertson (courtesy of the National Portrait Gallery, London).

In 1907 Ellen married James Carew, a young American actor who had come to the London stage a year earlier to forward his career. Ellen took Carew to America as her leading man and they were secretly married in Pittsburgh. Upon hearing of their marriage, G.B. Shaw, now safely married himself, said, "There, but for the grace of God, goes Bernard Shaw."

When Terry and Carew returned to London, they lived together in her Chelsea house. Carew loved her as much as any man in his thirties could love a beautiful woman pushing sixty, but recurrent rows and reconciliations, along with her daughter's rejection of him, doomed the marriage. Eventually they separated, but remained friends and never divorced.

Around the corner from Terry lived Charles Kingsley, who wrote *The Water Babies,* a classic read by every Victorian youngster. Continue along King's Road to Oakley Street and turn right. Follow Oakley Street south to Oakley Gardens.

10. Residence of Lady "Speranza" Wilde and Willie Wilde
87 Oakley Street

After several moves Lady Wilde finally settled here until she died in 1895. She was, perhaps, fonder of Willie than of Oscar, as Willie lived with her before and between his marriages. Willie was tall, bulky, bearded, vivacious, and so entertaining that one wealthy old lady paid him an annual salary of three hundred pounds just to visit her every afternoon and keep her amused for several hours. When he wasn't thus occupied, he worked as a journalist.

Unfortunately his Irish charm proved his undoing. A wealthy American widow, who had inherited a popular periodical, met him in London and decided that, as her husband, he would be a valuable asset to her journal. They married and immediately set sail for America. To her consternation, his ideas of marriage differed from hers. She had anticipated a quiet domestic life, but when they landed on the other side of the Atlantic, Willie couldn't understand why, since she was so rich, he should be expected to work. What America sadly lacked, he observed, was a leisure class—something he intended to rectify. While she sat home pining, he enjoyed jolly evenings with the boys—and sometimes the girls. Finally she divorced him. "He was of no use to me either by day or night," she told reporters.

Willie came home to Mama. Now Oscar was at the height of his fame—successful, in demand socially. Oscar had everything; Willie had nothing except a second-rate job on one of the newspapers. He took every opportunity to dig at his brother, even writing a disparaging notice of *Lady Windermere's Fan,* the hit show of the season. Oscar, although a little put out, simply shrugged and said, "After a good dinner one could forgive anybody, even one's own relations."

In 1894 Willie sobered up long enough to take another chance at marriage, this time to a pleasant woman named Lily Lees. It grieved Lady Wilde that so much enmity existed between her two sons, and she begged them to make up, to no avail. And then came a day between the infamous trials when no hotel would accept Oscar, and he, too, came home to Mama.

This was Willie's hour. His famous brother, fortune's darling, who had on occasion demonstrated his contempt for Willie's drunken habits and disreputable friends, was now at his mercy. Not one to let bygones be bygones, Willie sanctimoniously remarked, "Thank God my vices are decent ones!"

After Oscar's fall Lady Wilde went into seclusion, bearing his disgrace as if all Ireland were defying the universe in the person of her second-born son. Everyone else who knew and admired his talents urged him to escape before he went to trial. Money was presented and a yacht placed at his disposal, but Wilde could not be persuaded—perhaps due to his mother. "If you stay, even if you go to prison, you will always be my son," she said. "It will make no difference to my affection; but if you go, I will never speak to you again." She never spoke to him again in any event, as she passed away while he was in prison.

Wilde was in Switzerland recovering from his years in prison when he heard of his brother Willie's death in 1898—at the same time that he heard of the artist Beardsley's. Wilde suffered deeply over Beardsley's talent being snuffed at such an early age, but could not bring himself to mourn for his brother.

At Upper Cheyne Row turn off of Oakley Street and follow it the short distance to Cheyne Row.

11. Residence of George Gissing
33 Oakley Gardens

This controversial novelist lived in sometimes-shabby, sometimes-genteel poverty all of his life. His ill fortune was of his own making. He first married a prostitute who died, then another working-class girl, and he spent the last five years of his life living with Gabrielle Fleury, who translated his novels into French. He died in France in 1903.

While living in Chelsea, he wrote *The Unclassed,* a novel about exiles from society, a group with which he strongly identified. He would have received little sympathy from Wilde. "Misfortunes one can endure—they come from outside, they are accidents. But to suffer for one's own faults—Ah!— there is the sting of life," Wilde wrote in *Lady Windermere's Fan.*

Retrace your steps north on Oakley Street.

12. Residence of Thomas Carlyle
24 Cheyne Row

Known as the "Sage of Chelsea," Carlyle moved here in 1834 and remained until he died. His house had been built in the early eighteenth century, and Carlyle found it "a right old strong roomy brick house, likely to see three races of the modern fashionable fall before it comes down." But Cheyne

Row became increasingly busy, and he found the noise unbearable when he was trying to write; it even seeped in through the double walls he had constructed for his attic study. Jane, his wife, was knocked down by a cab in 1863 and died three years later. His niece, Mary Aitken, and her husband went to look after him for the last sad- and-silent fifteen years of his life. Like many famous writers, he shunned social life, once writing to his father, "Plenty of people come about us; but we go out little to anything like parties, and never to dinners; or anywhere willingly, except for profit." The house has been restored and now belongs to the National Trust, so it is open to the public.

Oscar Wilde's first trip to London, accompanied by his mother and brother Willie, was to celebrate his having passed the examination to win the Magdalen College demyship (scholarship) in classics. The trip resulted in visits to literary acquaintances of Lady Wilde's, so she could show off her brilliant son. They called upon Thomas Carlyle, whom Wilde later characterized as "a Rabelaisian moralist." However, after Carlyle's death, Oscar was proud to purchase his desk, expecting to find inspiration by using it.

Now continue south to Cheyne Walk (pronounced "chainy"), which runs perpendicular to Cheyne Row.

13. Cheyne Walk

This long, riverside walk is lined with houses overlooking picturesque bridges, and at the turn of the century was a haunt of London's most noted poets and painters. Today's poets might find it more difficult to hear "nature sing the exquisite song heard by artists alone" that so thrilled Whistler. We suggest this walk be scheduled for a Sunday, when traffic is reduced to a lull. If the day is foggy, all the better. Let your imagination concentrate on the scene of so many of Whistler's "impressions" and "nocturnes" as you listen to his words: ". . . when the evening mist clothes the riverside with poetry, as with a veil, and the poor buildings lose themselves in the dim sky, and the tall chimneys become campanili, and the warehouses are palaces in the night, and the whole city hangs in the heavens, fairyland is before us." Others besides Whistler captured Cheyne Walk's beauty, and consequently Chelsea became the center for an artist colony.

Battersea Bridge, an iron structure erected in 1890 which crosses the river at the end of Beaufort Street, replaced the picturesque old wooden bridge, which was a favorite subject with Whistler and other artists. The marvelous "cat's cradle" suspension bridge to the east is Albert Bridge, opened in 1873. On the corner of Cheyne Walk and Cheyne Row is King's Head and Eight Bells, a popular pub once favored by neighbors Whistler, Greaves and Carlyle.

There were so many outstanding residents on Cheyne Walk that we suggest you turn right from Cheyne Row and walk westward to Battersea Bridge. Then turn back and retrace your path along Cheyne Walk, continuing on to its east end as far as Tite Street.

14. Residences of James A. McNeill Whistler
101 and also 96 Cheyne Walk

This great American artist first took lodging here in 1862 while doing illustrations for *Once a Week*. Cocky and opinionated, he demonstrated right from the beginning a talent for alienating friends. A female admirer once asked him whether he thought genius was hereditary. "I cannot tell you, madam," he replied. "Heaven has granted me no offspring."

Only the road separated his house from the river, and he often painted the Thames from his window. Two doors from Whistler lived Greaves, a boat builder Whistler often used as a model, whose two sons would take him out in a boat any hour, day or night, to paint on the Thames.

A neighbor meeting Whistler on Cheyne Walk one day enthused, "I just came up from the country this morning along the Thames and there was an exquisite haze in the atmosphere which reminded me so much of some of your little things. It was really a perfect series of Whistlers."

"Yes, madam," Whistler responded gravely. "Nature is catching up."

He was the first artist to do night paintings. Mr. Leyland, a patron, suggested the name "nocturne." Whistler painted them for many years, but most were painted from his window. It was here that he resolved for himself that a painting should be a pattern of line and color independent of subject matter—not because it told a story or appeared lifelike, but because it was a thing of sheer beauty—a concept which differed from the current school of thinking in regard to art. He was very outspoken in his opinion that the detailed realism of Pre-Raphaelism was on the wane: "An artist should look at a flower not with the enlarging lens, that he may gather facts for the botanist, but with the light of the one who sees choice selections of brilliant tones and delicate tints, suggestions of future harmonies."

James A. McNeill Whistler, as painted by Sir Leslie Ward in 1878, (courtesy of the National Portrait Gallery, London).

Whistler had no real studio at this time, but created his Japanese-type paintings in a modest, little second-story back room. Paint was laid on thickly at first, but later more subtly. He was thrilled to finally sell one of his new paintings, until the buyer objected to his huge signature across its bottom. When he refused to change it, the sale fell through, although someone else soon bought it. Whistler never admitted defeat on the signature issue, but soon afterward he started interlacing his initials, Japanese fashion, into a more refined oblong or circular frame. Gradually the design evolved into a butterfly in silhouette and continued in various forms. Eventually the butterfly became the distinctive signature on all of his work, sometimes introduced into the design of a fabric or as a note of color, often appearing as a piece of decoration. Soon he was using the butterfly along with his signature to sign letters and invitations, until finally he used only the butterfly. In his book, *The Gentle Art of Making Enemies,* he used the butterfly as punctuation as well.

It was in 1864 that he painted *The Little White Girl,* which artists rank as one of the few great pictures of the world. Whistler painted her (his model and mistress, Jo) in a simple white gown, leaning against the mantel with her face reflected in the mirror. The room shows his blue-and-white Nankin china on the mantel. The girl holds a Japanese fan, and a spray of azaleas trails across her dress.

On a whim Whistler gave up his lodging to join with a group of friends, who left overnight to help fight an uprising in Valparaiso. After more misadventure than adventure, he returned to London in 1866 and moved into number 96 Cheyne Walk. This three-story house with an attic, part of a remodeled old palace, also looked onto the river.

On February 5, 1867 he threw a housewarming party. He had painted the dining room blue with a darker blue dado and doors, adding accents with purple Japanese fans tacked to the walls and ceilings. The beauty of the décor in all of Whistler's houses was its simplicity, an innovation when others were wavering between the riot of Victorian vulgarity and the overpowering opulence of Morris medievalism. He also had acquired a magnificent Chinese pagoda cabinet he was anxious to show off. (It is now displayed in the Leighton House museum in Kensington.)

In this house he continued to astound with his celebrated breakfasts. They began at 12:00 noon instead of 9:00 A.M. Nothing like them had ever been known in London. He sent invitations and arranged the table beautifully with his blue-and-white Nankin china, old silver, and a Japanese bowl of goldfish for a centerpiece. His menu was wholly bewildering to joint-loving Britons—the green corn and buckwheat cakes he sometimes called flapjacks were a sensation. Sometimes eighteen or twenty people sat down on packing cases, since he had only one chair, but more often he limited his guests to an exclusive eight or ten. Those invited were always distinguished royals or friends who were successful artists, actors and writers. Sometimes he would read out two or three stories of Bret Harte's—"The Luck of Roaring Camp," or "The Outcasts of Poker Flat." He also liked to recite Mark Twain's haunting jingle about the tramcar:

Punch—punch—punch with care
Punch in the presence of the passenger (jaire)

He was constantly in debt, and had bailiffs camped in his house, refusing to leave until paid. He fed them and ended up charming them into waiting table and helping out when he had guests, which was much of the time.

Whistler was a man who could never bear to be alone. His door was always open, and he liked to think that all doors were open to him. Lord Redesdale, who came to live on the Walk in 1875, said that Whistler was always running in and out, invited or not. At the same time a guest who once came to dinner in Whistler's house asked to stay overnight and remained for three years. He was a musician—a prince of parasites—but he amused Whistler and would accompany him on dark nights when he went out to paint his nocturnes.

Still, for all his hospitality, he was a snob. A notorious boor once approached him at a gathering and launched into conversation. "You know, Mr. Whistler, I passed your house last night . . ."

"Thank you," interrupted Whistler, and moved away.

During this period Whistler's straitlaced mother arrived unexpectedly from America. As the coach delivered her, a friend at the window sounded the alarm. Whistler's mistress, Jo Heffernan, was hilariously evicted out the window while his mother was walking in the door. The poor lady suffered many trials. Once she came into his studio to find the parlor maid posing in "the allover!"

She was patient, though, and posed serenely on his only chair for the *Arrangement in Gray and Black,* better known today as "Whistler's Mother," which now hangs in the Louvre in Paris. In 1872, however, it was refused by the Royal Academy in London, until strong objections from one or two members forced the committee to reconsider. It finally was hung in a poor place where groups gathered to laugh at it, as they had earlier laughed at his nocturnes. It was the last time he ever showed at the Academy.

15. Residence of Walter Greaves
104 Cheyne Walk

Son of a boat builder employed by J.M.W. Turner to row him across the river, Walter Greaves and his brother Henry lived near Whistler and they became close friends. Having been exposed to working artists all their lives, the brothers studied with Whistler, hoping to improve their own mediocre talents. Walter once pointed out that there was a basic difference in their attitudes toward boats: "Mr. Whistler put his boats in wherever he wanted them, but we left them just where they were . . . . to Mr. Whistler, a boat was a tone, but to us it was always a boat." Walter Greaves spent most of his life in virtual obscurity, but a few of his paintings became quite well known. One hangs in the Tate Gallery.

16. Residence of Hillaire Belloc
107 Cheyne Walk

This prolific poet, historian and essayist, who was born in France, moved to Chelsea in 1900, after Wilde had departed. Paradoxically described by contemporaries as both a "riveting conversationalist" and as a "dirty, noisy figure, an opinionated supertramp," he and Wilde would probably not have had much in common. He professed to be an intimate friend of novelist G.K. Chesterton's, but mutual friends observed that Belloc failed to turn up when Chesterton was received into the Catholic church. He did, however, attend the requiem for Chesterton in Westminster Cathedral, and in the course of the mass managed to sell an exclusive obituary of his friend to four different editors.

17. Residence of Wilson Steer
109 Cheyne Walk

Steer painted in his first-floor drawing-room studio here, but most of his time was taken up with introducing the work of French impressionists to England. A bachelor, he was inordinately proud of his collections of pictures, antiques, coins, bronzes and Chelsea porcelain, which filled the house. He lived more quietly than most of the other artists in Chelsea. Walter Sickert, George Moore, John Singer Sargent and William Rothenstein formed his regular circle.

18. Residence of Joseph Mallord William Turner
118 Cheyne Walk

This beloved English artist, the critic John Ruskin's favorite painter, was called "that old amateur" by his jealous, competitive neighbor, Jimmy Whistler. Turner, who lived here under the name of Booth, captured the enchanting light, as did Whistler, in a painting of Battersea Bridge from his window. Turner's landscapes are the star attraction of London's Tate Gallery's Clore Wing, which houses the Turner bequest.

When you come to the embankment on Cheyne Walk, continue eastward alongside the parking lot. Note the old iron Victorian postbox which still collects mail for Chelsea residents.

19. Residence of Dante Gabriel Rossetti and Algernon Charles Swinburne
16 Cheyne Walk

Rossetti, painter and poet, moved to Chelsea from Bloomsbury in 1862 and lived in this house he called "Queen's House" until he died. Earlier he had joined with John Everett Millais, Edward Coley Burne-Jones, William Holman Hunt and others to found the Pre-Raphaelite Brotherhood, typified by the sincerity in art which they believed had imbued the Italian painters before Raphael. In literature, especially in poetry, they made a similar attempt to follow nature and attend to the minutest details. Some of the best poetry of the time was printed in their journal, and a number of their paintings hang today in the Tate Gallery.

In 1860 Rossetti married his model, Elizabeth Siddal, whom he called "Guggums," but continued to see other women. After two years of marriage, Guggums gave up and killed herself with an overdose of laudanum. Rossetti was overwhelmed with grief. Many of his poems had been written for her. At the burial he wrapped the book containing the only copies of these poems in her long golden hair and consigned them to the grave. As the years passed, however, he began to think with regret of the poems, considering it was pointless to leave the finest work of his career to molder in the grave. After much business to obtain permission, he had the grave opened and retrieved his book. Its contents were published in 1870 under the title *Poems*. It was very successful. After Guggums committed suicide, Algernon Charles Swinburne, Edward Burne-Jones and George Meredith lived with him at different times.

Dante Gabriel Rossetti, self portrait of 1847, (courtesy of the National Portrait Gallery).

One day Rossetti announced that he wanted to buy an elephant. When asked what on earth for, he replied, "So I can teach it to wash the windows of my house," adding that then everyone would stare and say, "That elephant is washing the windows of the house in which lives Dante Gabriel Rossetti, the famous artist."

Any results of that novel idea are not recorded, but it didn't discourage Rossetti from filling his house and garden with other strange beasts—peacocks, a gazelle, a bull, monkeys, a Virginia owl, a Japanese salamander, hedgehogs and a sluggish pet wombat that came to the table to entertain guests. He used to talk to his bull. On one occasion the bull apparently took offense, pulled out his stake, and Rossetti barely escaped into his rear door, calling for his servant to come and tie up the beast. The servant was thoroughly exasperated. He'd gone about the house with peacocks tucked under his arms, he'd rescued an escaped armadillo from irate neighbors, and he had captured a monkey from the top of a chimney, but he was not about to tie up a mad bull.

He gave notice and resigned on the spot.

Whistler and Rossetti shared an interest in the spiritual, and their circle often held séances at Queen's House. On one occasion a cousin of Whistler's from the American South, long dead, told him of an incident that nobody else could have known about. It alarmed Whistler to the extent that he gave up spiritualism because he was beginning to find it so engrossing that it was taking his time away from painting.

Whistler and Rossetti also shared an interest in things Japanese, which Whistler had been introduced to while studying in Paris. They haunted galleries in search of blue-and-white Nankin china and Japanese prints, with which Whistler decorated his house. It was he who started the craze in England for oriental bric-a-brac and purity in design, which gradually replaced the overcrowded Victorian décor, where price was the measure of quality.

Even though Whistler had little respect for the Pre-Raphaelite Brotherhood, he and Rossetti remained neighbors and friends. On one occasion the feisty Whistler had engaged in a fracas with his brother-in-law in Paris, which had resulted in fisticuffs. On his return to London, he attended a dinner party given in his honor. Rossetti teased him with the following poem:

> *There's a combative artist named Whistler*
> *Who is, like his own hog-hairs, a bristler:*
> *A tube of white lead*
> *And a punch in the head*
> *Offer varied attractions to Whistler.*

The Pre-Raphaelite poet Algernon Charles Swinburne lived with Rossetti until he was taken in hand by his friend, Theodore Watts-Dunton, and moved to Putney Hill further out of the city. Swinburne was seriously ill from having led a dissipated life, and also suffered from a form of epilepsy.

When the poet laureateship fell vacant upon the death of Lord Alfred Tennyson, Swinburne was among the likely candidates to succeed him, but unlike the frustrated poetaster Sir Lewis Morris, he didn't take his chances seriously enough to campaign. (The eager Morris complained to Wilde, "It is a complete conspiracy of silence against me. What should I do?" "Join it," Wilde advised.) After a decorous period Queen Victoria appointed Alfred Austin.

Theodore Watts-Dunton, also a friend of the Pre-Raphaelites, had given up his career as a solicitor to become a critic, novelist and poet. He succeeded in stifling Swinburne's creative talents, but did satisfy some of the poet's more unusual desires. At The Pines, their house at Putney Hill, Swinburne liked to slide down the wooden banisters in order to experience the sheer pleasure of Watts-Dunton removing splinters from his posterior.

20. Residence of Mary Ann Evans (George Eliot)
4 Cheyne Walk

Born Mary Ann Evans, this novelist adopted a male name, believing that it would forward her career. She moved to Chelsea from Holly Lodge on the outskirts of London, where she had been living with a married man, the critic George Henry Lewes; thus she was a social outcast. She had written *The Mill on the Floss* there. Lewes died in 1878, and in 1880 George Eliot married John Cross, who, though twenty years her junior, had been an intimate friend of Lewes and herself. Cross took the lease on the Chelsea house before they married, but they spent only a short time there, as Eliot died in 1880. She had become a very wealthy woman in the 1870s after the success of *Middlemarch* and was acknowledged as one of the greatest novelists of the age.

Wilde once remarked that Eliot's style was cumbersome, but he didn't hesitate to poach her aphorism from *Middlemarch:* "Women are too poetical to be poets." Wilde's adaptation: "We Irish are too poetical to be poets; we are a nation of brilliant failures, but we are the greatest talkers since the Greeks."

Continue along the Chelsea Embankment to Tite Street and turn left. Like Cheyne Walk, Tite Street hosted a lively group of artists and writers, among them Augustus John, who lived at number 33 prior to moving to Mallord Street, and the frequent movers, Whistler and Wilde, both of whom had addresses here at various times.

21. Residence of Frank Miles and Oscar Wilde
3 Tite Street

Early in 1881 Wilde and Frank Miles quit their elegant quarters off the Strand at Salisbury Street and moved to Chelsea. Miles, who was supported by his father, a canon of the church, managed to coerce him into contributing enough cash to commission Edward Godwin, the architect who had done Whistler's White House, to redesign theirs on the same street. The design used interlocking rectangles of red and yellow brickwork, a roof covered in green slates, and windows with balconies. The result was an aesthetic pleasure. Wilde named it "Keats House," because two sisters named Skeates had occupied it before them, and Shelley House, occupied by a descendant of the poet, was just around the corner.

All went well for about a year; then Wilde published a small book of poems that shocked Miles's religious father to such an extent that he demanded Miles evict Wilde from the house. Since Miles was dependent upon the good canon for financial support, he acquiesced. The most shocking of the poems was "Charmides." Its theme was based on Wilde's memory of a classical Greek story about a young man embracing a statue of Aphrodite. Canon Miles was appalled. He considered the coupling with statues, suggested in the following lines, monstrous and sinful:

> And nigher came, and touched her throat, and with hands
> violate
> Undid the cuirass, and the crocus gown,
> And bared the breasts of polished ivory,
> Till from the waist the peplos falling down
> Left visible the secret mystery
> Which no lover will Athena show,
> The grand cool flanks, the crescent thighs, the bossy hills of
> snow.

An outraged Wilde retorted that his verse had larger purposes than to flatter the public. Moreover he had reason to suspect some hanky-panky between Miles and the very-young models he sometimes solicited—he was certainly suspicious enough to resent Miles's father's sanctimonious accusations of his immorality because of the poem. Wilde tore upstairs, flung his clothes into a large trunk, and tipped it over the banister, smashing an antique table. Then he swept out of the house, slammed the door, and never spoke to Miles again.

Some years later Miles's acts as a molester of children became public. He was arrested and later died in Brislington Asylum.

22. Residence of Constance and Oscar Wilde
34 Tite Street

Tite Street had not seen the last of Wilde. Some years later, flushed with success after his second American lecture tour and slightly richer, due to the dowry acquired by his marriage to Constance, the happy groom took a lease on number 34 Tite Street and commissioned architect E.W. Godwin and his friend Whistler to convert the interior of a commonplace Victorian house into a thing of beauty.

The walls of the dining room on the ground floor were white, blended with delicate tints of blue and yellow. The mantelpiece, carpet and chairs were also white. Wilde's study on the first floor had an Eastern flavor—oriental divans, Japanese prints, Moorish casements and numerous bookshelves. He only used this room for a smoking lounge, however, preferring to do his writing on the old Carlyle desk in a small downstairs room with buttercup walls, red-lacquered woodwork, a statue of Hermes and pictures by Monticelli and Simeon Solomon.

The drawing room was primarily Constance's domain. She chose faded brocades against a background of white and cream paint. Some of Whistler's Venetian studies lined the walls, and above a carved white mantelpiece was a huge gilt-copper bas-relief by Donaghue. On the opposite wall from it hung an oil portrait of Wilde by an American, Harper Pennington. Mounted on the ceiling were two many-hued Japanese feather fans, a typical Whistler accent.

Two sons were born to the Wildes—Cyril in 1885, and Vyvyan a year later. As time passed, Wilde spent less and less time at home. He once related to a friend how he had been telling his sons stories the night before about little boys who were naughty and made their mothers cry, and what dreadful things would happen to them unless they behaved better. "And do you know what one of them answered?" he marveled to his friend. "He asked me what punishment would be reserved for naughty papas who did not come home till the early morning and made mothers cry far more!"

Before much more time had passed, he was caustically citing such epigrams as: "When one is in love, one begins by deceiving oneself, one ends by deceiving others. That is what the world calls romance"; or, "In married life three is company and two is none."

23. Residence of John Singer Sargent
31 Tite Street

The famed American portrait painter and artist lived here for twenty-four years until he died, in this house that Whistler had occupied earlier. Sargent had studied painting in Florence and Paris. His first public success in England was *Carnation, Lily, Lily, Rose,* depicting children in a lovely garden lighting Japanese lanterns hung on trees. It was exhibited at the Royal Academy in 1887 and now hangs in the Tate Gallery.

Sargent became a royal academician ten years later, having gained an international reputation as a portrait painter. He was especially appreciated in Boston, where a number of his portraits hang on permanent exhibition. Among his celebrated portraits were one of Lady Londonderry, who dominated London society at the time, and Lord Ribbesdale's splendid likeness, that hung for many years on the stairway of Rosa Lewis's Cavendish Hotel in St. James's, where she used to raise her champagne glass and toast, "To Lordy—the greatest gentleman of them all!"

Sargent was indirectly responsible for Wilde's choice of Tite Street as a site for the house he built to live in with his bride. During the short period Wilde shared Tite Street quarters with Miles, he had witnessed Ellen Terry arriving at Sargent's nearby studio, costumed for his famous portrait of her as Lady Macbeth. Wilde wrote, "The street that on a wet and dreary morning has vouchsafed the vision of Lady Macbeth, in full regalia magnificently seated in a four-wheeler, can never again be as other streets; it must always be full of wonderful possibilities." Wilde was never one to pass up a possibility.

24. Residence of James A. McNeill Whistler
13 Tite Street

With the sale of a few paintings and an ambitious commission to decorate Leyland House in the offing, the dauntless Whistler hired architect Edward Godwin and proceeded to build a house he named the White House (now demolished) on Tite Street. It had facilities for printing and etching on the top floor and was the first of his houses to have a real studio. Lillie Langtry, Wilde, Frank Miles and countless other friends often gathered here for the famous breakfasts. Whistler loved his house, but Fate intervened in the form of the powerful critic, John Ruskin, who had "made" the Pre-Raphaelites and now set out to "unmake" Whistler.

Critiquing Whistler's painting *The Falling Rocket* (now in the Tate Gallery) in an 1877 show at the Grosvenor Gallery, Ruskin wrote that he had never expected to hear a coxcomb ask two hundred guineas for flinging a pot of paint in the public's face. Whistler sued him for libel and won a mere farthing, but he considered it a moral victory. The legal costs, however, combined with Leyland's refusal to meet costs on the elaborate decorating job, rendered him bankrupt. In September of 1879 Whistler fled to Venice. There he recapped his fortune with a series of brilliant etchings, but when he returned to London in November of 1880, art critic Harry Quilter had taken over his house and refused to give it up.

Whistler then moved into number 13, close to the White House, and a near neighbor to Wilde's and Miles's house. Here he reacted to his exile by deliberately wrapping himself for protection in malicious, extravagant wit and painting all of the fashionables—views of crowds competing for portrait sittings, carriages along streets. He resumed his Sunday breakfasts and again became a fashion setter with his blue-and-white china, old silver, and quixotic centerpieces. He invented amazing costumes, using a new fawn-colored, long-skirted frock coat, and he carried an extraordinarily long cane. The crowds came, but not the portrait sitters. To be painted by Whistler in the eighties required courage—it courted notoriety, if not ridicule. Lady Meux was the first to give him a commission, and two full-lengths of her are among his most distinguished portraits.

Until she became involved with the Prince of Wales, Lillie Langtry was a daily visitor. Whistler planned to paint her as *An Arrangement in Yellow*, a companion piece to the portrait of his mother, but they found other diversions and the work never progressed.

It was during this era that the two most grandiose egos and sharpest wits of London, Whistler and Wilde, discovered each other. One of their oft-quoted repartees followed the publication of an imagined conversation between the two in *Punch*. After reading it, Wilde sent Whistler the following telegram: "*Punch* too ridiculous. When you and I are together, we never talk about anything except ourselves."

Back came the reply from Whistler: "No, no, Oscar, you forget. When you and I are together, we never talk about anything except me."

But Wilde had the last word. "We may talk about you, Whistler," he agreed, "but I am thinking of myself."

Follow Tite Street north to Tedworth Square.

25. Residence of Samuel Langhorne Clemens (Mark Twain) 23 Tedworth Square

The famous American humorist lived here from 1896 to 1897. Before Samuel Langhorne Clemens took up writing and adopted the name of Twain, he had worked as a journalist and a river pilot on the Mississippi River, and had tried gold mining in Nevada during the Civil War. His novels, *The Adventures of Tom Sawyer* in 1876, and *The Adventures of Huckleberry Finn* in 1885, made him a fortune. He lived extravagantly, speculating in inventions which eventually left him bankrupt. He came to Europe in 1891 to earn money to pay his debts. After the death of his daughter Suzy in 1896, he led a secluded life in Tedworth Square, seeing only a few friends. The *New York Herald* started a public benefit fund to repay his debts, and Twain returned to America in 1897.

St. Leonard's Terrace, your next destination, lies next to Tedworth Square on the east.

26. Residence of Bram Stoker 18 St. Leonard's Terrace

Bram Stoker, the author of *Dracula,* moved to Chelsea in 1896, the year before *Dracula* was published. He wrote drama criticism for newspapers, and in 1878 joined Sir Henry Irving in the management of the Lyceum Theatre. Later, in 1906, Stoker published a biography of Irving.

Back in his Oxford days when he was twenty, Wilde had fallen in love with an "exquisitely pretty" seventeen-year-old girl named Florence Balcombe. He wrote love poems to her for several years and was seriously considering proposing when he received news that she was engaged to marry Bram Stoker. They remained friends, though, and the Stokers attended most of Wilde's opening nights.

Walk the short block north from St. Leonard's Square to King's Road, a major bus route that will get you to most destinations.

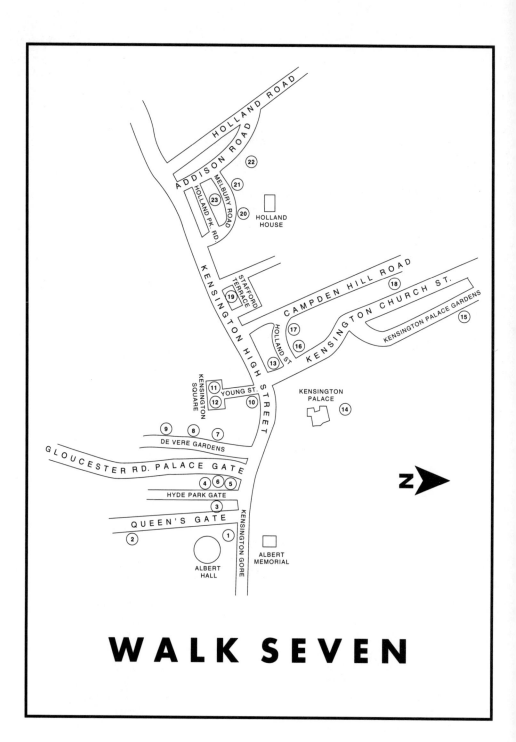

WALK SEVEN

Kensington Gore

For our purposes the Kensington Walk begins at the bus stop on the opposite side of Kensington Gore from the Albert Memorial, a monument commemorating Victoria's prince consort that resembles a gaudy Fabergé egg.

In 1846, when William Thackeray and his daughters moved into Kensington, his elder daughter described its main street as "a noble highway skirted by beautiful old houses with scrolled iron gates." Within a few years Kensington High Street had become a primary thoroughfare, busy with traffic and shops. Today it is a potpourri of the elite and purple-haired youths.

1. Residence of Sir Albert Sassoon
25 Kensington Gore

This once-magnificent mansion stands adjacent to a small plaza dominated by a statue of Lord Napier astride his horse. At the turn of the century, it housed the head of the Sassoon family, whose other members we met on the Mayfair and Belgravia walks. When the Sassoons moved their Bombay headquarters to London, company chairman Albert Sassoon followed his brothers Reuben and Arthur and acquired this house, that boasted two white-and-gold Louis XVI drawing rooms. He furnished the dining room with Jacobean furniture and a tapestry portrait of Queen Victoria. Woodwork in the house was carved and inlaid with ebony and ivory, which had been salvaged from the Prince of Wales's pavilion at the Paris Exhibition. At night, lamps of bronze gilt brought out the splendor of six immense tapestries depicting scenes from *The Merry Wives of Windsor.*

Sir Edward, Albert's son, married Aline de Rothschild from Paris and after Sir Albert retired to Brighton, they moved into this Kensington Gore mansion. Aline became influenced by Margot Tennant Asquith and joined the Souls, a coterie of wits and statesmen (whom we met at Margot's Cavendish Square home in Marylebone) formed to offset the raffish Marlborough House circle. When Sir Albert died, Edward succeeded to the baronetcy and became chairman of the firm. He had tired of Kensington Gore by then and bought an imposing mansion at 25 Park Lane near Rothschild Row.

Continue west on Kensington High Street. All of the following addresses, which are on streets as far west as

Young Street, are found a short distance to the left off Kensington. Most of the streets are cul-de-sacs. Weave a route among them by dipping down one side and returning on the opposite side to Kensington until you have reached Young Street.

2. Residence of Charlotte Payne-Townshend
21 Queen's Gate

Prior to her marriage to G.B. Shaw, Charlotte Payne-Townshend lived here with her mother and sister until her mother died. Then her sister Mary left home and Charlotte lived alone. When the two sisters were young, Mary was called Miss Payne-Townshend, and Charlotte, Miss Plain-Townshend. After Charlotte married Shaw, they lived in her Adelphi Terrace house that we visited on the Strand/Covent Garden walk.

3. Residence of Harry Cust
27 Hyde Park Gate

No sooner had this handsome devil emerged upon the London social scene than he became a most sought-after spare man. He could both quote the classics and get a difficult horse across the country. When the Souls' literary coterie dispersed, it did not slow Harry down. He continued to meet ladies of poetic persuasion by moonlight, starlight or sunset at their slightest inclination. He was a man who couldn't say "no."

Despite recurring dangers of scandal, he remained for several years a Tory member of Parliament. Men, as well as women, admired him. In 1892 William Waldorf Astor offered him the editorship of the *Pall Mall Gazette*. In spite of having no experience in publishing, he rallied such contributors as Rudyard Kipling, H.G. Wells, Arthur Balfour and others of literary renown, to the astonishment (and disappointment) of Fleet Street competitors.

Misfortune struck when Cust was on the verge of marrying a dazzling girl with a huge fortune. On a visit to Lady Horner, a highbrow hostess, he met Nina, the homely daughter of Sir William Welby-Gregory, a fourth baronet. His flattering attentions to the plain girl were misunderstood. She fell madly in love.

Determined to capture him, Nina wrote to Arthur Balfour and Lord Haldane, both high in government, saying that she was with child by Mr. Cust and that his anticipated marriage must be stopped. Balfour then prevailed upon him to marry her. In view of his devastating reputation with women, he had no recourse. But the story of the pregnancy proved unfounded. By strange and bitter chance, his wife turned out to be one of the few women who came under Harry's spell who did not bear him a child. He deserted Nina frequently, but she remained crazy about him. She studied sculpting and carved immense equestrian statues of Harry for her bedroom.

Harry gave her this large house (a new, unflattering front has been added), where they entertained his intellectual friends, but poor Harry went to his grave proving the truth of Wilde's epigram: "The happiness of a married man depends on the people he has not married."

After the Custs had given up the house, it was turned into a duplex and later occupied by Sir Winston Churchill, who died here in 1965.

4. Residence of Leslie Stephen and Julia Duckworth Stephen
22 Hyde Park Gate

Lady Julia and Sir Leslie were the parents of Virginia Woolf and Vanessa Bell. Sir Leslie's first wife was a daughter of William Thackeray's. After Julia and Leslie married, they moved into Julia's house, where he worked on his *Dictionary of National Biography* and entertained a host of writers, artists and musicians, among whom were George Meredith, Henry James, Edward Burne-Jones and George Watts.

Julia Stephen was exceedingly beautiful and sat for many artist friends as a favor. William Rothenstein, a protégé of Whistler's, was brought as a tea guest one day by a mutual friend. Awed by Julia's beauty, he had the temerity to ask her to sit for a drawing. When it was finished, she looked at it in silence, as did the rest of her family. Finally the word seeped upstairs to Mrs. Stephen's mother, a confirmed invalid. She had not left her room for many years, but on seeing the drawing, she rang for a cane and thumped heavily down the stairs to give the artist a piece of her mind. Whistler and his abstract technique was anathema in the Pre-Raphaelite, Burne-Jones and Watts circles.

Apparently Stephen outlived his prejudice, however. A 1903 chalk portrait of him by Sir William Rothenstein now hangs in the National Portrait Gallery.

5. Residence of Sir John Everett Millais
2 Palace Gate

While he painted in fits and starts, Millais lived in this grand mansion, still elegant today, where Sicilian marble covered the floors, and water spouted from the mouth of a black marble seal within a marble basin on the landing next to his forty-foot-long studio.

John Everett Millais, with his painting of Lillie Langtry as seen in Vanity Fair, *May 13, 1871. The caption reads, "A converted pre-Raphaelite."*

A Pre-Raphaelite painter, Millais first attracted attention with a painting called *The Carpenter's Shop,* in which he associated the Holy Family with the meanest details of the carpenter's life, omitting neither misery, dirt nor even disease, all of which were depicted with the same minuteness of detail. The painting was violently criticized, so gradually Millais changed into an artist more interested in pleasing than in educating his public, and became one of the wealthiest and most admired of Victorian painters.

His portrait of Lillie Langtry, called *The Jersey Lily,* was greatly praised and won honors. Like Lillie Langtry, Millais had also come from the British island of Jersey, which struck a common bond between them. It was in Millais's studio that Lillie Langtry first met Prime Minister Gladstone, who was sitting for the portrait that now hangs in the National Portrait Gallery. He was later to give her some good career advice.

When Wilde, while a relative newcomer to London, was favored with an invitation to a ball at Millais's home— probably due to his friendship with Lillie—he wrote to a friend at Oxford, "I am going with Ruskin to the theatre to see Irving as Shylock and afterwards to the Millais ball. How odd it is!"

It would have been even "odder" had John Ruskin been included in the invitation, since Ruskin had once been married to Effy, Millais's wife, until she had gotten an annulment because after five years, Ruskin had still been unable to consummate the marriage.

Paintings by Millais are well represented at the National Portrait Gallery, the Tate Gallery and Leighton House.

6. Residence of Frederick Leyland
6 Palace Gate

This hard-headed Liverpool shipowner was an admirer of Dante Gabriel Rossetti and purchased many of his paintings for his splendid art collection. Leyland also befriended Whistler and engaged him to do the decorating for his mansion. It wasn't an easy job. The walls had already been faced with leather, broken by a series of slender, vertical Gothic posts supporting shelves. While Leyland was in Liverpool, Whistler gilded the wood and overpainted the leather with sweeping, linear, Japanese-style peacock murals in blue, silver and gold. Nothing like the "Peacock Room" had ever been seen in London. Whistler made the mistake of showing it off in advance to everyone but Leyland.

When it was finished and Leyland finally allowed to see it, he was furious with Whistler for overpainting the leather and reneged upon the agreed fee, a factor which contributed to Whistler's bankruptcy. Nevertheless the house was Whistler's most-talked-about work, "a single experiment in decoration," according to the *Times* in 1877, "the ornamentation being entirely derived from the beautiful plumage of the peacock displayed in various forms." Whistler himself referred to it as a "Harmony in Blue and Gold."

7. Residence of Robert Browning
29 De Vere Gardens

The famed poet once confessed to Elizabeth Barrett Browning: "I myself am born supremely passionate—so I was born with light yellow hair." (I have yet to figure that one out, but that's what he said.)

He did not become well known as a poet until his return to London from Italy after Elizabeth's death in 1861, but eventually his reputation rivaled Tennyson's. His courtship of and elopement with Elizabeth resulted in a contented, artistically productive marriage, and he was desolate after her death. He returned to England with their young son, but later the winters found him increasingly ill, so he went back to Venice, where his son had settled. Browning was a frequent guest at Lady Wilde's soirées, and Wilde praised his writings during his lectures in America. When he died in 1889, he was buried in the Poets Corner in Westminster Abbey.

8. Residence of Henry James
34 De Vere Gardens

The American-born novelist, Henry James, lived in this five-story block of flats, now called Hale House, from 1886 to 1902. Many novelists of the time were drawn to the stage, James among them. His first play, *The American,* enjoyed a modest success. His second, *Guy Domville,* was a failure. Toward the end of the last act, Domville proclaims: "I am the last, my lord, of the Domvilles!"

"It's a bloody good thing you are," a voice shouted from the gallery.

The critics, too, were less than enthusiastic. James was mortified. "How can my piece do anything with a public with whom *that* is a success?" he cried, referring to Oscar Wilde's *An Ideal Husband,* which was playing at the same time.

James was born in New York, but after 1876, he settled in England and in 1916 became a British subject. During this period he wrote his diabolical story, "The Turn of the Screw," and turned from a popular, easily accessible novelist famous for his *The Portrait of a Lady,* to one admired by a small circle of readers willing to pursue his attempts to present "what goes on irreconcilably, subversively beneath the vast smug surface." James found his increasing isolation far from comforting: "I *have* felt, for a long time past, that I have fallen upon evil days—every sign or symbol of one's being in the least bit *wanted,* anywhere or by anyone, having so utterly failed."

9. Residence of Henry Morton Stanley
De Vere Gardens

The exact address is not on record, but in 1890, after his marriage, Henry Morton Stanley lived in one of the terrace houses in De Vere Gardens. Later he and his wife moved to a fine home at number 2 Richmond Terrace on the Victoria Embankment.

His real name was John Rowlands. He was brought up in a Welsh workhouse and in 1859 sailed to New Orleans, where he was adopted by a cotton broker, whose name he took. He fought on both sides in the Civil War and then took up journalism. In 1869 the *New York Herald* commissioned Stanley to find David Livingstone, who was lost in the African interior. He found him in November 1871 when, legend has it, he presented his card and said, "Dr. Livingstone, I presume?"

Stanley returned to equatorial Africa three years later and traced the course of the Congo. His final journey in 1887 was an attempt to rescue the Emir Pasha, but he failed and returned to London to live. He married Dorothy Tennant, sister of the incorrigible Margot Tennant Asquith, in 1890.

If you are looking for a change from pub food, Fox and Hendersons, on the corner of De Vere Gardens and Kensington High Street, serves a nice lunch or tea.

10. Residence of William Makepeace Thackeray
16 Young Street

Thackeray lived here until later moving to 36 Onslow Square. This comfortable, double-fronted family house proved a haven when he settled into it with his two young daughters, Anne and Minny. His wife had been insane for some years, and the girls had spent their early years in Paris with their grandparents. Anne later recalled how he would "write in the study at the back of the house. A vine shaded his two windows, which looked out upon the bit of garden, and the medlar tree, and the Spanish jasmine of which the yellow flowers scented our old brick walls . . . . the evening bells used to ring into it across the garden and seemed to come in dancing and changing with the sunset." Thackeray wrote *Vanity Fair* and *The History of Henry Esmond* here. Much of the action of the latter is set in nearby Kensington Square.

After his death on Christmas Eve, the girls remained in Kensington. Minny eventually married Leslie Stephen, who made it a *ménage à trois* with her sister Anne. When Minny died, leaving a retarded daughter for Leslie to raise, he then married one of his wife's best friends, Julia Duckworth (whom we met at their house a few blocks away on Hyde Park Gate.)

After Minny died, Anne stayed on to help Stephen until he remarried, but then they had a falling out over his disapproval of her affair with a cousin, Richmond Ritchie, seventeen years her junior. Their ultimate marriage shocked all connections, but the couple were supremely happy and rejoiced in their two children. Ritchie had a government career devoted to Indian affairs, while Anne distinguished herself with popular writing. Anne was elected to a fellowship in the Royal Society of Literature in 1903, and Ritchie was made a knight in 1907. Unfortunately he died comparatively young in 1912, preceding his wife's death by eight years.

Continue down Young Street to Kensington Square

11. Residence of Sir Edward Coley Burne-Jones
41 Kensington Square

A painter and designer, Burne-Jones was a Pre-Raphaelite and a William Morris disciple. His stained-glass windows of Gothic design embellish several London churches. He lived with Morris in Bloomsbury and later with Rossetti in Chelsea, until he could afford this five-story brick house with a southern exposure, overlooking the charming garden in the square.

During Whistler's lawsuit against John Ruskin, Burne-Jones evoked his enmity by siding with Ruskin, a strong Morris supporter. Aware of Wilde's intent to use Morris and his followers as champions of good design on his lecture tour in America, Whistler sent Wilde a message as he set sail: "If you get seasick, throw up Burne-Jones."

12. Residence of Mrs. Patrick Campbell
33 Kensington Square

Born Beatrice Stella Tanner, this impulsive actress eloped at the age of nineteen with Patrick Campbell, a minor city-office worker. Upon discovering her mistake, she turned to the theatre and made her triumphant debut as Paula Tanqueray in the first performance of Pinero's *The Second Mrs. Tangueray* in 1893. No other actress of her time could match her portrayal of passionate, complex heroines.

Her uncharacteristic (for her) romance by mail with G.B. Shaw continued for years. He admired her tremendously and created the role of Eliza Doolittle in his play *Pygmalion* for her. Prior to its opening this warning appeared in the *Daily Sketch:* "*Pygmalion* may cause a sensation. Mr. Shaw introduces a certain forbidden word. It is a word which the *Daily Sketch* cannot possibly print. And this evening the most respectable audience in London is to hear this appalling word fall with bombshell suddenness from Mrs. Pat's lips." The word was that old English epithet "bloody"!

When asked once by a pompous gentleman why it was that women were so devoid of humor, Mrs. Campbell responded, "God did it on purpose, so that we may love you instead of laughing at you."

After luring George Cornwallis-West away from his wife, the former Jennie Jerome Churchill, Mrs. Campbell finally settled again for "the deep peace of the double bed after the hurly-burly of the chaise longue" and married him.

Walk back up Young Street and cross Kensington High Street to Kensington Church Street.

13. St. Mary Abbot's Church
Kensington Church Street

At the altar here in August of 1888, Jimmy Whistler married the widow of architect E.W. Godwin, who had designed his beloved White House in Chelsea so many years earlier. Mrs. Godwin had studied art in Paris and was advanced enough in her appreciation to defend Whistler against press criticism of his art even before knowing him personally.

It was an unconventional courtship. Henry Labouchere brought the odd couple together after Mrs. Godwin was widowed, because they were both "bohemians." She, as large as Whistler was small, delighted him when he learned that there was Gypsy blood in her family. The attraction was obvious, but Jimmy, uncharacteristically shy, hesitated to ask her to marry him. So Henry Labouchere took them to dinner one night. When they were seated and imbibing an aperitif, Labouchere said, "Jimmy, will you marry Mrs. Godwin?"

"Certainly," he replied.

"Will you marry Jimmy?" he asked her.

"Certainly," she replied.

"When?" Henry asked.

"Oh, some day," Jimmy replied.

"That won't do," Labouchere said. "We must have a date." So they both agreed that Labouchere should choose a date, a church, a clergyman and give the bride away.

He fixed an early date and got them the then chaplain of the House of Commons. The wedding took place at St. Mary Abbot's in Kensington with Dr. and Mrs. Whistler, Jimmy's brother, one of Mrs. Godwin's sisters and a few friends in attendance. Labouchere gave the bride away, and Mr. Jopling-Rowe was best man.

Everybody needs friends like the Laboucheres. It was Henry's wife, Henrietta, who had coached Lillie Langtry and turned her into an actress when she was in desperate straits.

14. Kensington Palace

As you walk north on Kensington Church Street, the Kensington Palace gardens are on your right. The palace stands at the western edge of the gardens. It was the residence of the reigning sovereign until 1760, when George II died. Victoria was born here, as well as Queen Mary. Victoria learned of her accession to the throne here, and there is a statue of her by her own daughter, Princess Louise, outside, facing The Round Pond.

Today the palace is the London home of the Prince and Princess of Wales (Charles and Diana) and Princess Margaret. The state apartments, with an interesting collection of ladies' and gentlemen's court dress and uniforms displayed in period settings, are open to the public. There are also many fine paintings, dating from the eighteenth century to modern times.

Immediately behind the palace on the west side runs Kensington Palace Gardens, which extends into Palace Green at its south end. This wide, gated avenue of mansions built in the 1850s now houses embassies for the most part, or the residences of Middle Eastern potentates. The only personage connected with our era who lived here was Charles Brookfield, believed to have been the illegitimate son of Thackeray, who later took the name of his mother's husband. It makes the walk too long to include the whole complex, but you might want to take a peek at "Millionaires' Row" inside the gates.

15. Residence of Charles Brookfield
2 Kensington Palace Gardens

Brookfield was an actor and writer of burlesques. He happened to be playing in America when Wilde was on his first tour, and they met at a party. Wilde made the mistake of pointing out Brookfield's ill sense of propriety in keeping his gloves on at a tea party. Brookfield never forgave him. Later, back in London, Brookfield collaborated with Charles Hawtrey in goading Wilde, when they wrote a travesty of Wilde plays. Upon learning that Wilde's middle name was O'Flahertie, they began their piece, *The Poet and the Puppet,* with a song that ran in part:

> *They may bubble with jest at the way that I'm dressed,*
> *They may scoff at the length of my hair.*
> *They may say that I'm vain, overbearing, inane,*
> *And object to the flowers that I wear.*
> *They may laugh till they're ill, but the fact remains still,*
> *A fact I've proclaimed since a child,*
> *That it's taken, my dears, nearly two thousand years*
> *To make Oscar O'Flahertie—Wilde.*

Having suffered parodies in the past by Gilbert and others, Wilde was furious, but after appealing to the licenser of plays, Wilde won his point, only denying them the use of either "Oscar" or "Wilde." He did not object to the use of O'Flahertie, however, so the last line was altered to :

> *To make Neighbour O'Flahertie's child.*

Turn west onto Holland Street, a short distance north of St. Mary Abbot's Church.

16. Residence of Walter Crane
13 Holland Street

Crane wrote about his house: "After returning one day after a long and fruitless search for a house, my wife and I happened to pass along Holland Street and notice this house to let. It had an eighteenth-century brick front, which was attractive, and on entering we found, instead of the usual squeezy passage, a square hall with a fireplace. There was a garden at the back toward St. Mary Abbot's Church and on a fine old leaden cistern, there was the date 1674. The style of some of the moldings and woodwork suggested an earlier date." He lived and painted here until his death in 1915.

Crane had studied painting at the school of Mrs. Hume (Edith Dunn), along with Poynter, Nevinson and other London artists who later gained recognition. His name appeared often in Constance Wilde's guest book, and he was among the artists who signed a fruitless clemency petition for Wilde when he was imprisoned.

17. Elephant and Castle Pub
40 Holland Street

This is a delightful pub to stop in for refreshments, especially on a warm day when you can sit outside.

Holland Street runs perpendicular to Campden Hill Road. Turn right and proceed north.

18. Residence of Ford Madox Ford
80 Campden Hill Road

This lovely white house, set back from the street behind a wall hung with wisteria, was the home of the novelist and critic, born Ford Hermann Hueffer. Grandson of the Pre-Raphaelite painter Ford Madox Brown, and the son of Francis Hueffer, a well-known music critic, Ford changed his surname to Ford. He founded the *English Review* in 1908, whose early contributors included H.G. Wells, Henry James and John Galsworthy. His writing room was decorated in a violent shade of red by his friend Wyndham Lewis and was known as "the futurist's room."

In 1880, prior to Wilde's marriage to Constance, he had cause to entertain the idea that if married, he would be better able to confront society without having to affront it—a wife would save him from moralists—and a rich one from moneylenders. After Florence Balcombe, his first choice, preferred Bram Stoker, he then considered the beauteous Violet Hunt, young daughter of an artist and a novelist. Miss Violet was interested, but practicality got the best of her, and she fell in love with Ford Madox Ford, with whom she lived, unmarried, in this house.

Walk downhill to Kensington High Street and turn right. Then turn right on Argyll Road and left on Stafford Terrace.

19. Linley Sambourne House
18 Stafford Terrace

This little masterpiece of Victoriana is a museum managed by the Victorian Society. It was sold intact to the city of London by the Countess of Rosse, mother of Lord Snowdon and granddaughter of Mr. Sambourne, who built and furnished it in the 1870s. Sambourne was an illustrator and member of the staff of *Punch*. He entertained many artists, politicians and actors here. Some of his finest work appeared in his illustrations for *The Water Babies,* the Victorian children's classic which rests on a bed table in his house.

Unlike most London museums, which are free, there is a small fee to visit this one. The house has been beautifully maintained and is as typical an example of Victorian décor as can be found. Blue-and-white Nippon china still rests on dining-room shelves, the original Morris wallpaper covers walls, and cartoons and drawings by George Du Maurier, Walter Crane, and Luke Fildes hang along with Sambourne's own. This "middle-class" house is in interesting contrast to Leighton House, which awaits a few blocks away at the end of this walk.

The best way to reach Melbury Road from here is to turn left at the end of Stafford Terrace. Walk down to Kensington High Street and follow it westward the short distance to Melbury Road.

20. Residence of Sir Luke Fildes
11 Melbury Road

This dignified artist lived here from 1877 until his death. His son recalls his father's decision in 1875 to build a home and put into it all the money he had. The house would be designed by Norman Shaw, the most fashionable domestic architect of the day. Melbury Road was an extremely desirable location, as it is still. Norman Shaw called it "delicious." Sir Hamo Thornycroft, the sculptor, lived at number 2A, and artist Val Prinsep had commissioned Philip Webb to design his house and studio nearby. George Watts also was a neighbor and friend.

Fildes and his family moved into the house in 1877 (the plaque is incorrect according to his son). Every day at milking time cows came along the country lane from Holland House, through the gates into Melbury Road, and on to the dairy in Kensington High Street. Fildes's son recalls the William Morris wallpaper in the day and night nurseries, and Morris's black, spindly legged chairs with rush seats.

21. Residence of William Holman Hunt
18 Melbury Road

William Holman Hunt lived for many years in Chelsea, when he wasn't painting and traveling in the Middle East, but he spent his later years here and died in this house.

While organizing the Pre-Raphaelite Brotherhood with Millais and Rossetti, he shared a studio with Rossetti, and they often worked on each other's paintings. Rossetti would say, "Here, Hunt, you are best at hair. Do my hair and I'll paint that sleeve you're working on."

Hunt caught himself up in a "Pygmalion" plot when he fell in love with an ignorant urchin named Annie Miller, a product of the workhouse. After he cleaned her up, she became much desired as a model for some of his artist friends. Finally, when Hunt had sold enough paintings to pay his debts and realize his dream of traveling to the Middle East to paint, he left Annie in the charge of a Mrs. Bramah, who lived in Chelsea. This well-bred lady was commissioned to see to Annie's education in dancing, elocution and instructions in the social graces, so that when he returned, Hunt could be proud to present her as his wife.

After two years he returned to learn that she had been practicing dancing with his best friend Rossetti, and still could barely read or write. More smitten than ever with her improved appearance and manners, however, Hunt forgave her indiscretions and moved her to fancier quarters, supervised by a new tutor.

Now, while Hunt slaved over his easel to pay for all this and save enough to marry her, she practiced her newly learned charms in the Burlington Arcade, where she had the good fortune to meet the old rake, Lord Ranelagh, who contributed to her education in the ways of the world.

By this time Hunt's work was gaining recognition, but when he suggested marriage, Annie rebelled. She wasn't ready to give up her aristocratic lover. The guileless Hunt was distraught, until gossip of her betrayal seeped through to him. Then he generously paid off her debts and bid her a firm farewell.

But that wasn't the end of his trials with this lady. Ranelagh had no interest in supporting her, so he proposed that she sue Hunt for breach of promise, until Annie pointed out that then Hunt could introduce Ranelagh's name as the cause. Meanwhile young Thomas Ranelagh Thomson, the lord's cousin, was falling in love with her. To prevent a lawsuit that would involve his uncle, young Thomson cannily conceived a new scheme. If they held off until an opportune time, they could then produce Annie's trunk full of letters from Hunt, which might be worth something to the newspapers, if not to Hunt himself.

A time presented itself when the lonely Hunt settled for the very respectable Fanny Waugh as his bride. By now Annie was married to Lord Ranelagh's impoverished young cousin. The exposure of the letters would generate great embarrassment for the Waughs, as well as for Hunt, whose reputation as a "religious painter" was becoming well established.

Since the letters never were published, Hunt's friends assumed that he had succumbed to the blackmail and bought them back, especially when they eventually learned that Annie had been delivered of a daughter and was living very comfortably with her husband in Montrose House in Hampstead Heath.

Holman Hunt's paintings may be seen in the Tate Gallery.

Retrace your steps on Melbury Road the short distance back to where it meets Holland Park Road. This entire area was once the grounds of Holland House, an eighteenth-century estate. Little Holland House adjoined it, but was demolished long ago.

22. Site of Little Holland House

In 1863 the prominent artist G.F. Watts painted Ellen Terry and her sister Kate in Little Holland House, where he lived for many years as the houseguest of Mr. and Mrs. Thoby Princep. Princep was a former jurist in India, after which he had retired and become a member of the Council of India office in London. Mrs. Princep was ambitious to establish a "salon," but their house in Mayfair was too small. Through Watts they learned that Little Holland House, a farmhouse adjoining Lord Holland's own residence, could be rented. They leased it in 1850. Watts went to visit three days and stayed thirty years. The friendship endured as long as the Princeps had the house. It was demolished in 1875.

G.F. Watts, as seen in Vanity Fair, *December 26, 1891. The caption reads, "He paints portraits and ideas."*

Mrs. Princep built Watts up as a "resident artist," calling him "Signer." Her salon guests included Disraeli, Thackeray, Browning, Tennyson, Rossetti, Holman Hunt, Wilde, Gladstone, Lady Constance Leslie, Lady Somers, and others, among whom was one Tom Taylor, who introduced Ellen Terry to the resident artist when she was a young actress of fifteen, and Watts was a middle-aged bachelor of forty-seven.

Ellen had led a sheltered life, playing ingenue roles in the theatre with a troupe composed largely of her own family. Watts, enthralled with the beauty of Ellen and her sister, asked them to model. One of his finest works is the one of Kate, the sister. In the meantime he became infatuated with Ellen and one day kissed her. Impossible as it may seem in today's culture, innocent Ellen considered them engaged and actually thought herself pregnant because of the kiss. Watts, in turn, experienced an urgent need to protect her from the "dangers and temptations" of the stage, which pleased Ellen. She had been performing and on the road with her family from the time she could walk and had no interest in the theatre at that time. Her family was against her marrying a man so old, but when she confessed to her mother that she was having a baby, they became anxious to see it through. The two were married at St. Barnabes in Kensington on February 20, 1864.

Presumably Ellen didn't learn how babies were made even after her marriage. Although Watts was believed to be homosexual, he had practiced abstinence all of his life anyway, and most of his biographers believe this marriage was never consummated.

Watts moved Ellen into his quarters with the Princeps. During the first ten months of their marriage, Ellen gave up the stage and modeled for him constantly, sometimes until she fainted with fatigue. After that his interest waned, and her high-spirited youth started to annoy him. He suggested they separate legally. She moved back to her family and made a few stage appearances, until she fell madly in love and ran off with the young architect Edward Godwin, who later was to design the White House for Whistler (and whose widowed wife Whistler was to marry).

Ellen Terry's family ceased to receive her during the years she was "living in sin" with Godwin, and Watts, at that time satisfied with their legal separation, refused to grant her a divorce so she could marry Godwin and legitimize their children. In time, unfortunately for poor Ellen, Godwin drifted away and eventually married another lady, leaving Ellen an outcast from her family with two children to raise.

Meanwhile, at age sixty-nine, Watts found it advantageous to marry the rich Mary Fraser-Tytler, a formidable lady with artsy-craftsy inclinations, so he at long last divorced Ellen Terry. To support herself, she returned to the stage and purchased a residence in Earl's Court, West Kensington. Then, to make peace with her family and as a concession to respectability, she impulsively married an alcoholic actor named Charles Kelly, expecting to reform him. After a few fretful years, she sent him on his way.

Her children still had not been blessed with a surname. At that point Ellen simply selected the name of Craig from a landmark rock called Ailsa Craig, and had both of her children christened with the name—Edy became Edith Geraldine Ailsa Craig and Teddy became Edward Henry Gordon Craig. The actor Henry Irving, Ellen's leading man for over twenty years (separated from his wife, but never divorced), was godfather for both children. Ellen Terry at the end of her career was covered on the Chelsea walk, where she moved from Kensington.

At the end of his life, Watts became known as the grandest of the "grand old men of British art." His reputation did not hold up with time, however. Although the Pre-Raphaelites returned to favor, Watts's work remains relatively unknown, in spite of some fine portraits by him in the National Portrait Gallery.

23. Residence of Lord Frederick Leighton
12 Holland Park Road

This noted Victorian painter and sculptor deigned to sculpt Lillie Langtry's head when they met on the event of her first social appearance in London. Leighton prided himself on his thorough draftsmanship. Meeting Whistler one day on Piccadilly, he remarked upon the other artist's technique: "My dear Whistler, you leave your pictures in such a crude, sketchy state. Why don't you ever finish them?"

"My dear Leighton," was the response, "why do you ever begin yours?"

Leighton, as opposed to Whistler, introduced a classical revival into Victorian painting. In 1866 he employed George Aitchison to build Leighton House to reflect his unusual and exotic tastes. The Arab hall was an authentic copy of a hall in Moorish Spain, the dome inlaid with stained glass, and the walls faced with tiles collected by Leighton and his friends from the Middle East, Rhodes and Persia. Contemporary artists added to the decorations. Walter Crane designed the mosaic frieze of the white stone staircase leading to the domed landing, and Randolph Caldecott, the birds on the marble columns supporting the dome. Leighton became president of the Royal Academy in 1878. He died the day after he was raised to the peerage.

His house, now a museum and gallery of paintings by Leighton contemporaries, is the highlight of the Kensington walk. The Arab hall, with the lull of water tinkling against myriad tiles, and prisms of color dancing in the bay of the fountain, makes you love the man simply for having conceived it. Here one easily imagines a caftan-robed Holman Hunt and others of Leighton's exotically inclined friends lounging on silk ottomans, sipping thick Turkish coffees, perhaps smoking water pipes, and trading dreams.

After Leighton House, anything else is anticlimatic. Major bus connections may be made a block away on Kensington High Street.

WALK EIGHT

BLOOMSBURY

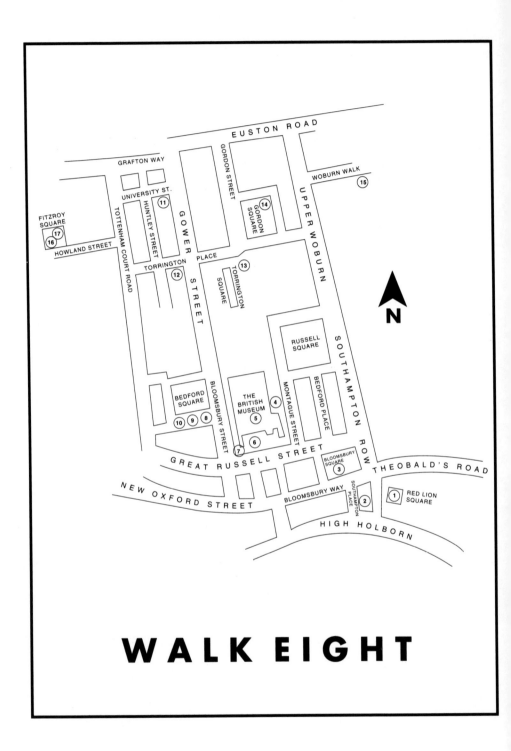

WALK EIGHT

Bloomsbury is the heart of intellectual London. Both the British Museum and London University are located here, together with publishing houses, bookstores, art galleries, and small museums. As a conclave for intellectuals, it reached its zenith during the decade or two following Wilde, with the ascendance of writers Virginia Woolf, Lytton Strachey, Wyndham Lewis, E.M. Forster, Clive Bell and others of the artistic tradition, who, like the earlier Souls of Wilde's time, formed themselves into a clique called the Bloomsbury Group.

The district's name is a corruption of the word *Blemonde*. In the eleventh century the land was given by William the Conqueror to his vassal, Baron Blemonde. Today's Bloomsbury had its beginnings in 1660, when the Earl of Southampton laid out a square south of his house. The Duke of Montague built a lavish mansion on the site of the present British Museum. To the west the dukes of Bedford and other great land-owning families established residences. Their family names—Russell, Tavistock, Bedford and Woburn—still label the area. In the eighteenth and nineteenth centuries, this was an elegant neighborhood of handsome row houses and attractive squares. Gradually it became less desirable, although still respectable. Eventually the mansions became flats and small hotels, occupied by students, artists and intellectuals.

Streets here are crowded with serious-looking scholars and professors, hurrying to classes or perusing books on the green lawns of spacious squares. Bloomsbury is a distinctive sector of London, perhaps more appealing to the academician than to the layman.

Southampton Row

This area may be reached both by a High Holborn bus to Southampton Row, or by underground to Holborn Station. Follow the map east from Southampton Row to Red Lion Square.

1. Residence of Dante Gabriel Rossetti, Walter Deverell, William Morris and Edward Burne-Jones
17 Red Lion Square

Although this building is unimposing, a lot of creative living took place in it. Before moving to Chelsea (where we have already heard about him), poet and painter Dante Gabriel Rossetti shared a studio on its first floor with fellow artist Walter Deverell. Rossetti's noted *Beata Beatrix,* as well as other of his Pre-Raphaelite paintings rendered here, feature Elizabeth Siddal, his model and mistress, whom he called "Guggums" and later married.

In 1856 when Rossetti moved, artists William Morris and Edward Burne-Jones took over the studio. Morris, who called himself "the idle singer of an empty day," created furnishings for their rooms with medieval designs of knights and ladies painted upon them. He was an apostle of the cult of art critic John Ruskin, who taught that the art and architecture of which he approved (mostly Gothic) would bring redemption from the sins of the Victorian world, that had fallen from grace by worshiping the machine.

William Morris by Abel Lewis, c. 1880, (courtesy of the National Portrait Gallery, London).

Morris manifested his faith by carrying this influence into mundane articles like furniture and wallpaper design, the ultimate outgrowth of which was art nouveau. His conviction that proper interior design depended upon hand-crafted articles designed to compliment each other established his reputation as a designer in every phase of décor, and ultimately proved such a commercial success that he obtained number 8 Red Lion Square in 1861 and opened Morris, Marshall, Faulkner & Company. Later his style was so popular that a posh outlet of Morris & Company opened at 449 Oxford Street, and even today original Morris designs enhance expensive wallpapers.

Wilde was an admirer of Morris—first for his poetry, and later for the art-and-craft revival Morris stimulated with his designs. During Wilde's "Decorative Arts" lectures in America, he deplored work he saw in the Philadelphia School of Design, where young ladies painted moonlight upon dinner plates and sunsets on soup plates. In delivering his message to America that "bad art is worse than no art," Wilde drew heavily upon Morris as a good example.

In 1865 Morris moved the headquarters of his firm to 26 Queen Square, where he worked and lived until he died in 1896.

Sir Edward Burne-Jones, a pre-Raphaelite painter greatly influenced both by Rossetti and Morris, is best known today for the stained-glass windows he designed, among them one in Holy Trinity Church on Sloane Street in Belgravia. Burne-Jones was friendly with Wilde and exchanged a number of letters through the years. Immediately upon Wilde's fall, however, he urgently requested that Wilde's friend, Robert Ross, see that all of his correspondence with Wilde be returned to him.

Return the short distance to Southampton Row, and cross it to Southampton Place.

2. Residence of Cardinal John Henry Newman
17 Southampton Place

Cardinal Newman, the Anglican who helped found the Oxford Movement and later, in 1845, joined the Roman Catholic church, lived in this Georgian house named Newman House, a short distance to the west of Red Lion Square. Here, as a boy, he used to play in nearby Bloomsbury Square with his playmate, Benjamin Disraeli. After his conversion Newman founded the impressive oratory in Brompton Road. At one point in 1877, when Newman had returned to Oxford to receive an honorary fellowship, Wilde entertained a dream of visiting him to convert to Catholicism, take the holy sacrament and gain quiet and peace for his soul, but the mood soon passed, and Wilde took no action until many years later on his deathbed.

Cross Bloomsbury Way to Bloomsbury Square.

3. Residence of Benjamin Disraeli 6 Bloomsbury Square

Benjamin Disraeli, Earl of Beaconsfield, was born in 1804 into a distinguished, relatively prosperous family. Shortly after his birth the family moved from 22 Theobald's Road to

Benjamin Disraeli, the Earl of Beaconsfield, in 1879.

Bloomsbury Square. In 1817 his father left the Jewish faith and had all of his children baptized in nearby St. Andrew's Church. Disraeli grew up in the Church of England and remained a staunch member for the rest of his life. As a Christian, he was free to embark upon a public career, at that time closed to Jews due to the Test Act.

At an early age Disraeli wrote, "Personal distinction is the only passport to the society of the great." Already he had determined that political power and prestige in Parliament constituted the only fit career for a gentleman not born to aristocracy.

At an early age, also, he discovered the value of a socially influential woman. His earliest conquest was Sara Austin, a married lady with social pretensions, who kept a salon at nearby 33 Guilford Street off Bloomsbury Square. Sara, twelve years his senior, appreciated the opportunity to prove her faith in his talents by arranging for the publication of *Vivian Grey,* his first novel with political overtones. Her faith paid off—for Disraeli, anyway. The novel was a huge success and launched his political career, of which we have already heard on the St. James's walk.

From Bloomsbury Square follow Great Russell Street to Montague Street, which runs along the east side of the British Museum.

4. Residence of Sir Arthur Conan Doyle
23 Montague Street

Sir Arthur Conan Doyle of Sherlock Holmes fame lived here when he arrived in London to practice medicine, and first met Oscar Wilde. Although in later years Doyle noted an extraordinary change in Wilde and thought he had gone mad, his earlier impression was one of intense admiration. At that time, as an unsuccessful doctor and almost unknown author, Doyle had come to London to dine with a representative of his American publisher, Lippincott. A fellow guest was Oscar Wilde, who immediately put Doyle at ease by praising his *Micah Clarke,* which had just been published.

Wilde's conversation left an indelible impression on Doyle. To illustrate the commonly held view that the good fortune of one's friends makes one discontented, Wilde wittily devised the following parable:

The devil's agents were trying to enrage a holy man whose composure remained unruffled. The devil, who happened to be passing, witnessed the failure of his agents and decided to teach them a lesson. "What you do is too crude," he admonished. "Permit me for one moment."

He then approached the holy man and said softly, "Your brother has just been made Bishop of Alexandra." Instantly the good man's countenance was distorted by an expression of jealousy and vindictive fury.

"That is the sort of thing I should recommend," advised the devil to his agents.

Many a successful person has lamented the truth of that parable.

As a result of the meeting, Doyle wrote *The Sign of Four* for Lippincott, and Wilde wrote *The Picture of Dorian Gray*. (Before moving his fictional Sherlock Holmes to lodge with Dr. Watson at 221B Baker Street, Doyle had him living on Montague Street.)

5. The British Museum
Great Russell Street

The British Museum holds the world's greatest collection of antiquities. During Wilde's early period of preoccupation with Greek art, he was fond of saying that a head like Lillie Langtry's could only be found on the silver coins of Syracuse. Later, after meeting Sarah Bernhardt, he enlisted Lillie's help in searching among the Greek coins in the British Museum for one with Bernhardt's profile.

There is a typical English story told about an apparent suicide in the British Museum. It concerns the death of one Henry Symons, a sometime deputy superintendent of the reading room, who shot himself in the Cracherode Room. According to the story his superior's first comment on hearing the news was, "Did he damage the book bindings?"

In the mid 1800s Karl Marx moved with his family to London. Desperately poor, they shared a house with a number of other families. In order to find quiet, Marx spent most of his waking time in the British Museum, where he worked on *Das Kapital*.

6. Site of Randolph Caldecott's Residence
46 Great Russell Street

While engaged as the illustrator for Washington Irving's books, Randolph Caldecott took rooms in 1872 opposite the British Museum, not because he loved the city, but because he felt: "London is the proper place for a young man, for seeing the manners and customs of society and for getting a living in some of the less frequented grooves of human labour; but for a residence, give me a rural or marine retreat." Consequently he escaped the city during his summers abroad, where he went seeking inspiration for his work.

The building is now an antique bookseller's shop.

7. Residence of George Du Maurier
91 Great Russell Street

George Du Maurier, artist and writer, lived at this address above the offices of Pears Soap between 1863 and 1868. He began working for *Cornhill Magazine* as an illustrator and produced some of his finest designs for Mrs. Gaskell's novel, *Wives and Daughters: An Everyday Story.* Later, as his work changed to reflect a commentary on fashionable society, he turned from artist to journalist and became a permanent member of the staff of *Punch.*

While an art student in Paris, Du Maurier had lived with the expatriate American artist, Jimmy Whistler. The sight of his old friend as a constant companion to Wilde stirred him in 1881 to create his hilarious caricatures of two aesthetic types, the poet Maudle and the painter Jellaby Postlethwaite. Week after week these caricatures appeared, never mentioning Whistler, who was too distinguished to be an easy target, but constantly featuring Wilde, with his flowing locks, his lilies, his blue china and his poems entitled "Impressions." If not always clever, the parody was good-humored, and Wilde was too aware of the usefulness of publicity to quarrel with *Punch.* Whistler, on the other hand, grew envious of the attention Wilde was getting. Upon seeing Wilde and Du Maurier talking together one day, he cried out in a jealous rage, "Which of you two discovered the other?"

Wilde generously replied, "We have both discovered you." The soft answer did nothing to diminish the irascible Whistler's wrath. Thus the Victorian era's two most colorful characters drifted apart, as Wilde's presence and wit gradually usurped the older Whistler from his coveted position as "king" of any social event at which he was present.

George DuMaurier, depicted in 1896 by Sir Leslie Ward,
(courtesy of the National Portrait Gallery, London).

Later in life Du Maurier moved to a magnificent house in Hampstead Grove and began to write novels based on his student days in Paris. *Trilby* was a best seller and subsequently a success on the stage for the actor/producer Herbert Beerbohm.

Turn right onto Gower Street and follow it north.

8. Residence of Sir Johnston Forbes-Robertson 22 Bedford Square

The west side of Gower Street is one of London's longest unbroken stretches of late-Georgian houses. Just past Gower Mews, turn right into Bedford Square, a gracious square with nicely kept row houses, gas lamps and tall trees. It was the second square to be built in Bloomsbury, unique because of its circular garden within the square and its broad promenade of paving stones. The scent of old roses and heather that fills the air, and the expansive grass area within wrought-iron gates, remain as unaltered today as the eighteenth-century houses that surround the square.

Sir Johnston Forbes-Robertson, among the first of the knighted actors.

Under the guidance of Henry Irving at the Lyceum Theatre, Forbes-Robertson's *Hamlet* was acclaimed as the greatest theatrical performance of the late 1890s. His noble bearing and fine character were instrumental in leading the way for other actors, playwrights and producers to be knighted. Forbes-Robertson did much to raise theatrical standards, both as an actor and a manager.

9. Residence of Sir Anthony Hope Hawkins
41 Bedford Square

Another resident of the charming square was this dignified barrister-turned-novelist, who used his experience to create Ruritania in his classic, *The Prisoner of Zenda*.

10. Residence of Margot Tennant Asquith
44 Bedford Square

This colorful lady, who was introduced on the Marylebone walk, lived her last years in Bloomsbury. When close to seventy, she decided to learn how to drive a car. Luckily for the safety of others, the fancy did not last long. For the event, however, she characteristically appeared dressed in breeches and a flying helmet.

Return to Gower Street and continue north.

11. Marlborough Arms Pub
Gower and University streets

This atmospheric pub, enhanced with old brass lamps and walnut paneling, and as popular with students as with faculty, features a typical pub lunch of cottage pie, English sausages or jacket potatoes with various stuffings. After numerous visits it remains one of our favorites.

12. Dillon's Bookstore
Gower Street and Torrington Place

A block from the pub is Dillon's Bookstore, created from a series of little shops designed by the architect to the Bedford estate in 1898. We consider it one of the finest bookshops in all of London.

Follow Torrington Place east to Torrington Square.

13. Residence of Christina Georgina Rossetti
30 Torrington Square

Poet and sister of Pre-Raphaelite artist Dante Gabriel Rossetti, Christina wrote her verses under the pseudonym Ellen Alleyne and often modeled for Rossetti's paintings depicting allegorical subjects, some of which may be seen in the Tate Gallery. Profoundly religious herself, she rejected proposals from both John Collinson and Charles Cayley because they did not share her High Anglican beliefs, which may have motivated the hopeless tone of her poetry, which was devoted to the agonies of unfulfilled love.

Nearby, on the corner of Torrington Place and Gordon Square, stands Christ Church, which holds a reredos painted by her brother's friend, Edward Burne-Jones, to commemorate Christina.

Return to Torrington Place and proceed north to Gordon Square.

14. Residence of Lytton Strachey
51 Gordon Square

The most impressive of Bloomsbury residential squares today, Gordon Square housed a number of the intellectuals embraced by the Strachey clique, among them Virginia Woolf and literary hostess Lady Ottoline Morrell. Strachey, noted critic, biographer and leading member of the set, had an apt answer for visitors who imposed upon his leisure. Some time had passed since a former visit by a rather noisy young man who once had been his houseguest. When they met again, the young man said, "Mr. Strachey, do you realize it's five years since we met?"

"Rather a nice interval, don't you think?" Strachey replied.

At the urging of Sir Herbert Beerbohm, when he managed the Haymarket Theatre, Oscar Wilde wrote *A Woman of No Importance.* Critic Lytton Strachey considered it the weakest of the plays Wilde wrote in the nineties, but he reluctantly agreed with the enthusiastic audience that in it the characters utter some of Wilde's wittiest epigrams. In the play Lady Allonby is a conscious wit and a match for Lord Illingworth when he remarks: "The Book of Life begins with a man and a woman in a garden." She retorts, "It ends with Revelations."

Another line from the play is frequently quoted by modern environmentalists opposed to hunting: "The English country gentleman galloping after a fox—the unspeakable in full pursuit of the uneatable."

Some years later Strachey built his reputation as a writer with the publication of his *Eminent Victorians,* a book depicting the era's bourgeois society.

During World War I he chose to appear before a military tribunal as a conscientious objector. The chairman's stock question was, "Tell me, Mr. Strachey, what you would do if you saw a German soldier trying to violate your sister."

"Try to get between them," Strachey replied, a response which greatly amused those aware of his homosexual proclivity.

From Gordon Square proceed in a northeasterly direction to Upper Woburn Place and look for Woburn Walk, an atmospheric, alleylike street with old gas lamps and eighteenth-century shop fronts. On a warm day the little coffeehouse here provides a shady retreat.

15. Residence of William Butler Yeats
5 Woburn Walk

This Nobel Prize-winning Irish poet and dramatist, steeped in Eastern religions and mysticism, was described, when he was seventy years old, by writer Vita Sackville-West as "a handsome man who has no small talk, but who either remains silent or else plunges straight into the things that matter to him." Guests to Yeats's chamber in Woburn Walk found it gloomy until their eyes adjusted to the dim room, lit by tall church candles in portly Italian blown-glass flasks, placed on low black-lacquered bookcases. Black velvet hung from the ceiling to the black-carpeted floor, accented by white wall spaces only wide enough to set off his erotic Aubrey Beardsley drawings. Yeats himself wore a belted jacket with a flowing tie and a broad ribbon trailing from pince-nez eyeglasses that made of his long face what one of his friends described as "an insect mask."

Among those attending his popular Monday "at homes" were George Moore, John Masefield, Rupert Brooke, Ezra Pound and Lady Gregory. They referred to themselves as "the tragic generation," with a creed that held "an opposition to all ideas and all generalizations that can be explained and debated."

In his younger days, when Yeats first moved from Ireland to London, his father deplored his association with Arthur Symons, a young ballet enthusiast and poet whom he feared might introduce young Yeats to "a chorus girl." The effete "new youth" of that era fancied themselves burdened with causeless disillusionment. It was Symons who, at age twenty-four, wrote:

> *What joy is left in all I look upon?*
> *I cannot sin, it wearies me. Alas!*
> *I loathe the laggard moments as they pass;*
> *I tire of all but swift oblivion.*

In spite of the pseudosophistication of England's educated youths, Yeats's father had little to fear. To his peers the young man often claimed that conversation was more important to him than sex and apparently held to that belief even in maturity. "Men don't talk well to each other," he later avowed. "They talk well to women. There must be sex in good talk . . . a man has no ideas among men—but he goes home to a cook or a countess and he is all right."

Among the "good talkers" Yeats romanced was his first unrequited love, the beautiful Irish nationalist, Maud Gonne. After a mournful period he rebounded into a torrid affair with Olivia Shakespear, a married woman. He asked her to leave home with him, but she wanted to wait until her mother died. After that event she asked her husband for a separation, but he became ill, and she decided it would be kinder to deceive him. To accommodate discretion, Yeats moved into number 18 of the Woburn Building with Olivia's help. While they were choosing their furniture, an embarrassing interlude occurred with a man in a shop concerning the width of their bed. Following that exposure, the romance slowly cooled, and soon the vacillating Olivia was replaced by another great love of Yeats's life, the comely actress Florence Farr, who inspired his play, *The Land of Heart's Desire.*

Florence's assets must have been more than purely vocal, however. The sexually reticent George Bernard Shaw, from whom Yeats stole Florence, claimed that only twice in his life had he been sexually infatuated—once as a youth and once in middle age. The youthful fling had been with Florence Farr.

Yeats, a frequent guest when Lady Wilde (Oscar's mother) entertained her Irish friends, was among the first to hear Wilde's "The Decay of Lying," a successful dialogue inspired by a conversation with his friend and disciple, Robert Ross. Enormously impressed by Wilde's hard brilliance and dominating self-possession, Yeats commented that he envied those men who can become mythological while still living. "I think a man should invent his own myth," Wilde replied. (Indeed he did!)

Shaw once wrote of Yeats, "He is not a man of this world, and when you hurl an enormous, smashing chunk of it at him, he dodges it, small blame to him."

From Upper Woburn work your way west to Grafton Way, which leads into Fitzroy Square on the outer fringe of

Bloomsbury. It is rather a long walk. If you wish to stop at this point, Euston Road is on a major bus route and only one block north of Upper Woburn and Woburn Walk.

16. Residence of George Bernard Shaw
9 Fitzroy Square

Fitzroy Square, like Bedford Square, is graced with a circular garden within the square and a broad, gas-lamp-lit promenade, set with old bricks and paving stones. Robert Adams, the famed architect, lived here, and the designs of the houses reflect his dignified style, in contrast to the gimmicky Victorian buildings prevalent in other parts of the area. Note the old mud scrapers at the entrances to houses, and the black iron hitching posts that surround the fenced garden in the center of the square.

Shaw carried on his romance by mail with Ellen Terry from this house on the square until he was lured to the altar at age forty by Charlotte Payne-Townshend, a "green-eyed Irish millionairess," and moved to her house in the Adelphi. He had written numerous unpublished novels prior to finally gaining recognition as a critic. His first plays, written in the 1890s, shocked their audiences by examining prostitution, male chauvinism and slum landlords.

His rooms here were cluttered with books, which he never closed, but laid one upon another. Servants gave up trying to keep order among the mounds of buried books, all wide open and stained with congealed remnants of meals. When he moved from Fitzroy, Virginia Woolf took over his flat.

As a young man embarking upon his literary career, Shaw met Wilde, then at the height of his fame, in the rooms of a mutual friend. Shaw told the company about a magazine that he intended to found, speaking with such enthusiasm that his Irish brogue became increasingly evident. Eventually Oscar Wilde interrupted to say that Shaw had not told them what the magazine would be called. "Oh, as for that, what I'd want to do would be to impress my own personality on the public. I'd call it *Shaw's Magazine*. Shaw, Shaw, Shaw!" he went on, pounding the table.

"And how would you spell it?" inquired Wilde.

Isadora Duncan, the early advocate of free love and modern dance, once wrote to advise Shaw that good eugenics indicated they should have a child together. "Think of it! With my body and your brains, what a wonder it would be."

"Yes," Shaw replied, "but what if it had my body and your brains?"

In spite of numerous "sexless" affairs, Shaw considered himself a romantic, explaining that he identified genius with immunity from the cravings and turpitudes which make us human. Hence his regime of sexual continence which so dismayed the women he loved, and hence, too, his abstinent diet of grated vegetables.

George Bernard Shaw photographed by F.H. Evans, (courtesy of the National Portrait Gallery, London).

Max Beerbohm, writer and contemporary of Shaw, observed that as a teacher and propagandist, Shaw was no good at all, but as a personality, he was immortal.

17. Residence of Marquess Robert Gascoyne Cecil of Salisbury 211 Fitzroy Square

Salisbury was the first statesman to hold the offices of prime minister and foreign secretary at the same time, and the last prime minister to sit in the House of Lords. The death of this deeply conservative aristocrat marked the end of the Victorian age in British politics.

Ordinarily the honorable marquess was a bit too conservative for the Prince of Wales, although Salisbury's expertise came in mighty handy during a *liaison dangereux* with Lady Daisy Warwick and Lord Beresford, which we have already heard described on the Belgravia walk.

From Fitzroy Square, walk a short distance north to Euston Road, a major bus route which will carry you to your chosen destination.

EPILOGUE

In the introduction to this book, we identified four personages as the style setters of the late-Victorian era—Oscar Wilde, James A. McNeill Whistler, Lillie Langtry and the Prince of Wales. So what happened to these lustrous personalities when the romantic nineties came to an end?

Oscar Wilde, photographed in 1891 by W & D Downey—before his fall from Grace.

We find Oscar Wilde self-exiled in France, a ruined man, a thwarted genius, reliving the horrors of his two years in prison as he writes his last masterpiece, "The Ballad of Reading Gaol." Lines from it:

And the wild regrets, and the bloody sweats,
None knew so well as I:
For he who lives more lives than one
More deaths than one must die.

When asked why he wrote no more after that, he replied, "I wrote when I did not know life; now that I do know the meaning of life, I have no more to write. Life cannot be written; life can only be lived. I have lived."

Wilde died on November 30, 1900 at the age of forty-six in his room at the Hôtel d'Alsace in Paris. His remains were put to rest at Bagneux but later moved to Pére Lachaise, when the famous funerary monument by Epstein was placed in 1909. It bears an inscription from "The Ballad of Reading Gaol":

And alien tears will fill for him
Pity's long-broken urn,
For his mourners will be outcast men,
And outcasts always mourn.

Constance Wilde, who had changed her name to Holland and moved to the continent with their two children, died in 1898. She and Wilde never met again after his release from prison.

Wilde's Salomé, which had been considered too risqué to open in London when Bernhardt attempted to produce it there, became a Max Reinhardt production at the Kleines-Theatre in Berlin after Wilde's death. It established him as a European writer of note, and his works began to sell in over a dozen languages. His bankruptcy was soon annulled, all his debts paid, and by 1908 his estate was in flourishing condition. Up to World War II, Wilde was more widely read on the continents of Europe and Asia than any writer in English except Shakespeare.

Picture Lillie Langtry, now Lady de Bathe, majestically strolling through the casino at Monte Carlo, while her young husband gamboled and gambled with skinny, flat-chested flappers so different from the overblown beauty she had been in her day.

Actually Sir Hugo de Bathe, called Shuggy, rather amused her, when she bothered to think of him. Lillie lived happily in her lovely Monaco hillside house with a devoted secretary/companion, Matilde Peate, while Shuggy lived uneasily some distance away in fear that Lillie might divorce him, thus cutting off his allowance and inhibiting his exuberant life style.

But that, she would never have done. During her reign as a social figure, it had rankled that she was the only commoner (untitled) person in her aristocratic set. Almost immediately upon Edward Langtry's death, she had married Shuggy. At last Lillie was a lady.

The stage had never been her ambition; it had merely offered itself as a means to an end—independence. In retirement on the Riviera, she addressed gardening with the wholehearted zest she earlier had devoted to the theatre and to her racing stable, and was awarded first prize by the Horticultural Society for the best garden grown by an amateur. "Small successes sometimes please out of all proportion," she said in response to her award. "In younger days the recognition would not have meant so much. Today it reflects the sheer pleasure I get from still feeling vitally alive."

Lillie, lamentably, was never reconciled with her daughter, but she did get to know her four grandchildren, who were allowed to visit on occasion. She died in her Monaco villa on February 12, 1929 of a heart attack brought on by influenza. She was seventy-six years old.

James A. McNeill Whistler died in London on July 16, 1903 at age sixty-nine. Recognition had finally come to him in his later years, especially on the Continent. He was awarded a membership in the Munich Academy, the Cross of the Order of St. Michael, an LL.D. from Glasgow University, the Legion of Honor, and a gold medal at Paris, where he and his wife lived for much of their ten years of marriage. After her death he lost some of his jauntiness, although to one patron who complimented him on a painting, saying it was the finest work of the sort since Velázquez, he unabashedly drawled, "Why drag in Velázquez?"

That paragon of sartorial splendor, the Prince of Wales and later King Edward VII, died on May 6, 1910, leaving a trail of romantic memories and amorous letters (some of which later appeared in print). While Britain mourned, perhaps the best summation of his royal career is found in Wilfrid Scawen Blunt's diary notation written on May 20, 1910, the day the king was buried: "Edward VII's particular qualities—his showmanship, his diplomatic achievements, his conscientiousness—doubtless made him a wiser and a better King than most of ours have been, and he may even rightfully share with Solomon the title of the 'Wise.' They each had several concubines and, as we know, 'The knowledge of women is the beginning of wisdom.' It teaches tolerance for the unwisdom of others."

His wife, the long-suffering Queen Alexandra, was heard to say as he lay on his deathbed, wheezing with bronchitis, "At least now I know where he is."

His Majesty, King Edward VII.

ACKNOWLEDGEMENTS

First and foremost I am indebted to my husband Denis Thompson. Denis has lived in London most of his life, and it would have been all but impossible to design these walks without his help. He routed the maps, reread copy countless times and made valuable suggestions.

We wish to thank our friend Jim Teevan from Hillsborough, California, who walked with us every step of the way, and whose wit and enthusiasm contributed to the pleasure of our work. Other friends, Shirley Beck and Carol Elliot, were kind enough to lug my broken computer back from London, a real test of friendship.

We are enormously indebted to the superb library in Coronado, California, that at times ordered special books for us, and to the Salt Lake City Library for the contributions it made to our research.

We are grateful for the encouragement and help of family and friends, too many to mention individually, but we especially wish to thank Marian and George Anderson, and Lynda and Stephen Thompson in England; Betty and Hal Ansel in Coronado; Emily and Trent Lowe in Salt Lake City, and Betty Charette of Seattle for research on Lillie Langtry. I would also like to commend the artist Ming Lowe from Palm Desert, California, for her penetrating impression of Oscar Wilde.

BIBLIOGRAPHY

Aronson, Theo. *The King in Love.* London: John Murray Ltd., 1988.

Benet-Dodd, Laura. *Enchanting Jenny Lind.* New York: Dodd, Mead & Co., 1954.

Birkett and Richardson. *Lillie Langtry.* Dorset, England: Society Jersiaise, 1979.

Blunt, Wilfrid Scawen. *My Diaries: Being a Personal Narrative of Events 1884-1914.* London: 1921. Reprint. New York: HippocreneBooks, 1980.

Brough, James. *The Prince and the Lily.* New York: Coward McCann and Geoghegan, Inc., 1975.

Brown, Craig and Cunliffe, Lesley. *The Book of Royal Lists.* New York: Summit Books, 1982.

Carr. *Some Eminent Victorians.* London: 1908.

Collis, Maurice. *Nancy Astor.* New York: E.P. Dutton and Co., 1960.

Cornwallis-West,George. *Edwardian Hey-Days: Or a Little About a Lot of Things.* New York: G.P. Putnam & Sons, 1931.

Crosland, Margaret. *Colette: The Difficulty of Loving.* London: British Book Center, 1954.

Ellmann, Richard. *Wilde and the Nineties.* Princeton: Princeton University Press, 1966.

Ellmann, Richard. *Oscar Wilde.* New York: Vantage Books, 1984.

Fitzhugh, Harriet. *The Concise Biographical Dictionary of the Famous.* New York: Grosset and Dunlap, 1950.

Fleming, G.H. *Victorian Sex Goddess.* New York: Oxford University Press, 1990.

Gerson, Noel. *Lillie Langtry.* London: Robert Hale and Co., 1971.

Haight, Mary Ellen Jordan. *Walks in Gertrude Stein's Paris.* Salt Lake City: Peregrine Smith Books, 1988.

Hibbert, Christopher. *The Horizon Book of Daily Life in the Victorian Age.* New York: American Heritage Publishing Company, 1975.

Holland, Vyvyan. *Son of Oscar Wilde.* London: Thames and Hudson Ltd., 1955.

Holland, Vyvyan. *Oscar Wilde.* London: Thames and Hudson Ltd., 1966.

Holman-Hunt, Diana. *My Grandfather: His Wives and Loves.* New York: Norton, 1969.

James, Henry. *Autobiography.* Edited by Frederick Dupee. Princeton: Princeton University Press, 1983.

Jullian, Philippe. *Oscar Wilde.* New York: Viking, 1969.

Jenkins, Roy. *Victorian Scandal.* New York: Chilmark Press, 1965.

Langtry, Lillie. *The Days I Knew.* New York: George H. Doran Co., 1925.

Lawton, Mary. *Queen of Cooks—And Some Kings.* New York: Boni & Liveright, 1924.

Le Gallienne, Richard. *The Romantic Nineties.* New York: Doubleday, 1925.

Leslie, Anita. *The Marlborough House Set.* New York: Doubleday, 1973.

Maugham, W. Somerset. *A Writer's Notebook.* New York: Doubleday & Co., 1949.

Morton, Frederic. *The Rothschilds.* New York: Atheneum, 1962.

Pearson, Hesketh. *G.B.S. A Full Length Portrait.* New York: Harper and Brothers, 1942.

Pearson, Hesketh. *Oscar Wilde, His Life and Wit.* New York: Harper and Brothers, 1946.

Pedrick, Gale. *Life with Rossetti.* London: MacDonald Ltd., 1964.

Pennell, Joseph and Pennell, Elizabeth R.. *The Life of James*

McNeill Whistler. 2 Vols. Philadelphia: J. B. Lippincott Co., 1908.

Pepper, Frank S. *The Wit and Wisdom of the Twentieth Century: A Dictionary of Quotations*. New York: P. Bedrick Books, 1987.

Robertson, William Graham. *Life Was Worth Living*. New York: Harper and Brothers, 1931.

Russell, Henry. *Sayings of Oscar Wilde*. London: 1989.

Sichel, Pierre. *The Jersey Lily* New York: Prentice-Hall, Inc., 958.

Skinner, Cornelia Otis. *Madam Sarah*. Boston: Houghton Mifflin Co., 1967.

Sutherland, Douglas. *The Yellow Earl*. London: Cassell, 1965.

Sykes, Christopher. *Nancy: The Life of Lady Astor*. Chicago: Academy Publications, 1972.

Terry, Ellen. *The Story of My Life*. New York: McClure Company, 1908. Reprint. New York: Schocken Books, 1982.

Von Eckardt, Wolf, et al. *Oscar Wilde's London: A Scrapbook of Vices and Virtues 1890-1900*. N.Y.: Doubleday, 1987.

Von Gleichen-Russwurm. *Dandies and Don Juans*. London: Knopf, 1927.

Wilde, Oscar. *The Complete Works of Oscar Wilde*. 15 vols. New York: Lamb Publishing Co., 1909.

Wilde, Oscar. *Writings of Oscar Wilde*. New York: Wm. H. Wise & Co., 1931.

Winwar, Frances. *Oscar Wilde and the Yellow Nineties*. New York: Harper and Bros.,

INDEX

Index to the works of Oscar Wilde
    mentioned on these pages: